*San A*

# the Pursuit of Equal Education

## DATE DUE

| | |
|---|---|
| NOV 1 4 2013 | |
| | |
| | |
| | |
| | |
| | |
| | |
| | |
| | |
| | |
| | |
| | |
| | |
| | |

# LANDMARK LAW CASES

## AMERICAN SOCIETY

Peter Charles Hoffer
N. E. H. Hull
*Series Editors*

PAUL A. SRACIC

# San Antonio v. Rodriguez and the Pursuit of Equal Education

## The Debate over Discrimination and School Funding

UNIVERSITY PRESS OF KANSAS

© 2006 by the University Press of Kansas
All rights reserved

Published by the University Press of Kansas (Lawrence, Kansas 66045), which was
organized by the Kansas Board of Regents and is operated and funded by Emporia
State University, Fort Hays State University, Kansas State University, Pittsburg State
University, the University of Kansas, and Wichita State University

Library of Congress Cataloging-in-Publication Data

Sracic, Paul A.
San Antonio v. Rodriguez and the pursuit of equal education : the debate over discrimination and school funding / Paul A. Sracic.

p. cm. — (Landmark law cases & American society)
Includes bibliographical references and index.
ISBN 0-7006-1483-4 (cloth : alk. paper) — ISBN 0-7006-1484-2 (pbk. : alk. paper)   1.
San Antonio Independent School District — Trials, litigation, etc.   2. Education —
Finance — Law and legislation — United States.   3. Educational equalization —
Law and legislation — United States.   4. Discrimination in education — Law
and legislation — United States.   I. Title.

KF228.S26S73 2006
344.73'076 — dc22      2006019966

British Library Cataloguing-in-Publication Data is available.

Printed in the United States of America

10 9 8 7 6 5 4 3 2 1

The paper used in this publication meets the minimum requirements of the
American National Standard for Permanence of Paper for Printed Library Materials
z39.48-1992.

# CONTENTS

U.S. constitutional law has a fascination amounting to obsession with categories — the little supposedly airtight boxes into which each case fits, and the confines of which dictate how every opinion will be shaped. So cases with as convoluted social and political contexts and consequences as *Brown v. Board of Education* (1954) neatly fit into the box of the Fourteenth Amendment marked "Equal Protection." A state or its agencies could not mandate segregation of the races in its public schools because this violated the Equal Protection Clause. One would think that *Brown*'s penumbra, with its far-reaching shadows, would encompass the right to an education for persons of Mexican American ancestry. Not so, as Paul Sracic demonstrates in this deeply moving and richly told tale.

It began with a funding formula for public schools in Texas that returned to rich districts ample monies, and denied to poor school districts anything more than the basic necessities. On its face, this seemed fair, because public education was based on real estate tax formulas, and even if the mill levy was set at the same percentage level for all districts, wealthy districts would provide a higher dollar amount for their schools.

Nor was discrimination against Mexican American children formally based on race. Texas did not segregate Mexican Americans (as it did African Americans). Nevertheless, informal real estate arrangements insured that Mexican Americans would end up in barrios, and the drawing of school district lines effectively segregated Mexican American children in their own schools.

In the end, a realistic look at the situation would have immediately revealed that the impact of Texas school funding law was to discriminate against Mexican Americans. But would the law respond to reality, or cling to its little boxes? Despite long-standing legal abuse, each generation of Mexican American parents and children looked to the law to gain a fair shake. The legislature, however, refused to adopt various reform plans. Finally, in 1968, Demetrio Rodriguez and six other parents filed suit in federal court seeking an order requiring the state to develop some plan for equalization of funding.

Sracic tells the rest of this story with clarity and fair-mindedness.

He explores how the plight of the children touched a chord in the academic community, how the petitioners joined with a courageous local attorney to pursue the case and gained the ear of the nation, and how the legislature dragged its feet. Victory seemed within the petitioners' grasp as they gathered evidence of the disparate impact of the funding formula on their children's futures. When the state appealed the district court opinion, a new set of players entered the rolls — led by the "education justice" Lewis Powell. His role in the U.S. Supreme Court's hearing of the case was crucial.

*San Antonio v. Rodriguez* would become a landmark case for the issues it raised and the way in which the courts responded. Although the High Court continued to regard funding for public education as a local matter unless it was racially biased on its face, putting it in a different box from state-sponsored segregation, forces gathered within states to press the case for equal funding under state constitutional provisions. Then, and only then, would no child be left behind.

For the story it tells, San Antonio v. Rodriguez *and the Pursuit of Equal Education* is a lesson in the limits of purely judicial solutions to blatantly discriminatory educational conditions. It is also a lesson in how to write that story. Sracic brings together oral history, litigation, and constitutional law in the tale of a community that sought legal redress against great odds. If its effort did not bring immediate rewards, Sracic's effort could not have been more successful.

As has been the case with almost everything that I have written, this book emerged from my classroom lectures. For more than a decade now, I have been teaching classes in law and government at Youngstown State University. Whether I am teaching a basic introductory American government class or a more advanced course on constitutional interpretation, I always cover the "two-tier" approach to the Due Process and Equal Protection Clauses of the Fourteenth Amendment. The reason is obvious: students cannot hope to comprehend very much about how the third branch of the federal government, the U.S. Supreme Court, decides constitutional cases if they are not familiar with this approach and closely related terms such as "strict scrutiny" and "rational basis." This is particularly true with regard to the types of cases — abortion and affirmative action, for example — with which undergraduates are likely to be already familiar when they walk into class.

In any type of instruction, examples are helpful. Indeed, one of the benefits of teaching classes in law and government is that real world illustrations of abstract concepts are readily available. As I suspect is the case in many college classrooms around the country, when I teach students about the two-tiered approach I always rely on *San Antonio v. Rodriguez* (1973) as my "sample case." There are several reasons for this. First, the general subject matter of the case — the funding of primary and secondary schools — involves institutions with which virtually every student is likely to be familiar. Moreover, in Ohio, where I teach, as in a majority of the states, school funding cases are continually before courts and in the news. Most importantly, however, *Rodriguez* helps to answer the one question that seems always to occur to attentive undergraduates: "Can you give us an example of an ordinary or nonfundamental right?" The surprise that usually crosses the students' faces when the answer "the right to an education" is given speaks volumes about the importance of the case.

Although there is a plethora of commentary on both Justice Lewis Powell's majority opinion in the case and Justice Thurgood Marshall's dissent, very little has been written about the history behind the case. A few articles did appear in the year or so following the decision, and

Peter Irons included two chapters on *Rodriguez*, including an interview with Demetrio Rodriguez, in his book *The Courage of Their Convictions*. Still, many questions remain. Why, for example, did this case arise when it did? Is it significant that the case involved Mexican Americans? Why, in light of *Brown v. Board of Education* (1954), was the notion of a "right to an education" dismissed? These and other questions were always in the back of my mind as I laid out the cold facts of the case to my students. This is why, when Michael Briggs, editor-in-chief of the University Press of Kansas, asked me to suggest a case for the "Landmark Cases" series, *San Antonio v. Rodriguez* was one of the first cases that came to mind.

This book is organized in a way that allows the reader to gain the background information necessary to understand the more complex discussions that follow. In Chapter 1, before going into the details of the *Rodriguez* case, I offer a general introduction to the history of education in the United States, paying particular attention to the intersection of education, wealth, race, and politics in this country that forms the foundation to the legal case. Chapter 2 builds on this introduction, focusing on the events and legal decisions that immediately preceded the filing of the case. The discussion of cases continues in Chapter 3, where I explain the political and legal context of *Rodriguez*, emphasizing the transition between the Warren and Burger Courts as well as the development of the all-important two-tier equal protection test. Finally, I move to a specific discussion of the case. Chapters 4 through 8 take the reader step-by-step through the legal proceedings in *Rodriguez*, culminating in a summary of the various opinions in Chapter 9.

There are two main legacies of *San Antonio v. Rodriguez*. First, in deciding that there was no fundamental constitutional interest in education and that wealth was not a "suspect classification" under the Fourteenth Amendment, the Court in *Rodriguez* perhaps inadvertently encouraged more litigants to bring education cases to state courts under state constitutional provisions. This situation, along with many of these cases, is explained in Chapter 10. Beyond educational funding, however, *Rodriguez* also represents a turning point in the Court's understanding of the demands of the Fourteenth Amendment's Equal Protection Clause. Since cases that involve similar constitutional principles are not isolated from one another based on the specific issues involved, the jurisprudence established by Powell's *Rodriguez* opinion influenced the outcome of other noneducation funding cases. In Chapter 11, I discuss this legal phenomenon and provide examples from school bussing as well as abortion funding cases to illustrate *Rodriguez*'s impact. Finally, in Chapter 12 I briefly draw together my observations, evaluating *Rodriguez*'s relevance to modern debates about U.S. education.

The result, I hope, is a book that will interest a wide variety of readers. Lawyers, judges, and citizens interested in constitutional law will gain some insight into a case that has served as a precedent for many of the controversial decisions handed down by the Supreme Court over the past thirty years. Academics and students of the Supreme Court as an institution will find in this book evidence of how the background of justices — in this case, Justice Powell's service on the Richmond and Virginia Boards of Education — is reflected in their approach to constitutional interpretation. Finally, those who follow the ongoing political fights and litigation over how to fund schools might enjoy learning about the historical foundations of the school funding debate. I expect that everyone will come away from this book — as I have from the research and writing — with a healthy respect for the complexity of school funding both as a political and legal issue.

There are many people who deserve to be recognized for the help and encouragement they have given me while I have worked on this book. I am, of course, grateful to Michael Briggs, editor-in-chief at University Press of Kansas, for being open to a proposal about a case that is fairly obscure among those who do not study law and the Supreme Court. Throughout the process, he has been encouraging, optimistic, and understanding. One could not ask for more from an editor.

It would have been difficult if not impossible for me to pursue an academic career if not for the support (financial and otherwise) of my parents, Albert and Elizabeth Sracic, and of my wife, Susan. Over the past three years, Susan and our two daughters, Katya and Anna, have had to live with the project as much as I did. Indeed, they even learned what I suspect every author would like all his or her associates to know: never to ask how the book is "coming along." For this and other gifts, I am in their debt.

I have benefited from having outstanding academic mentors. More than twenty-five years ago, on my first day as an undergraduate at

Albright College, Thomas Brogan was assigned to me as my academic advisor. This is a role that I have never really allowed him to abandon, and he has never failed to provide support and guidance as I have pursued my career as a political scientist. In graduate school at Rutgers University, I was fortunate to discover yet another lifelong teacher, Wilson Carey McWilliams. Sadly, Professor McWilliams passed away while I was completing this book. Nevertheless, I doubt this book would ever have been written — at least by me — if I had not walked into Professor McWilliams's classroom some eighteen years earlier. Through both his words and actions, Professor McWilliams taught me not just about the study of politics, but about how to study politics. It is perhaps not a coincidence that when I began looking into the background of this case, the first book I turned to was *North from Mexico*, written by Professor McWilliams's father, Carey McWilliams.

Sunil Ahuja, William Eichenberger, Keith Lepak, and David Porter, my colleagues in the Political Science Department at Youngstown State University, have always been encouraging, and have provided valuable feedback as I worked on this project. William Binning, the only department chair with whom I have ever worked, deserves particular thanks for allowing me to design a teaching schedule that would accommodate my research and writing goals, and for supporting my application for the sabbatical leave during which the proposal and initial research for this book took place. Finally, I would like to thank Linda Babinec, the secretary in the Political Science Department at Youngstown State University, along with Megan Graff, who served as my research assistant. Ms. Babinec was always available to proofread chapters, type necessary correspondence, photocopy material, and in general, listen to me talk about "the book." Ms. Graff is one of the most capable undergraduates I have ever met. Her ability to read, highlight, and summarize complex cases and articles was nothing short of amazing, and saved me hours of time.

Finally, I received a University Research Council Grant from Youngstown State University in 2003 that allowed me to spend time at both the Manuscript Division of the Library of Congress and at the Lewis Powell Archives at Washington and Lee University.

# CHAPTER I

# Education, Wealth, Race, and Politics

The headline on the front page of the March 22, 1973, edition of the *Washington Post* consisted of a simple declarative statement: "Property Tax Use on Schools Upheld." Of course, headlines are of necessity brief and intended only to give the reader a rough sense of the story that follows. Even by such forgiving standards, however, this headline, although technically accurate, was hopelessly incomplete.

The article went on to describe the Supreme Court's decision in the case of *San Antonio Independent School District v. Rodriguez*. The facts of the case are fairly straightforward. Like every state except Hawaii, Texas funded its public schools, at least in part, through the imposition of local property taxes. The result was predictable: School districts containing an abundance of high value property were able to generate more money for their schools than districts that lacked property wealth. In the *Rodriguez* case, Demetrio Rodriguez and six other parents of children who attended school in the poor, overwhelmingly Mexican American Edgewood section of San Antonio filed suit in federal court arguing that the Texas funding system violated the Equal Protection Clause of the Fourteenth Amendment to the U.S. Constitution. As the headline noted above makes clear, the parents did not ultimately prevail.

The basic "facts" of *Rodriguez*, however, do not provide much of a clue to its real significance. Recently, the *Curiae Project*, based at the Yale University Law Library, attempted to rank the most commonly cited Supreme Court cases based on whether the opinions issued by the Court are given primary treatment in fifteen prominent constitutional law textbooks. The study found that *Rodriguez* was among only a handful of cases that received mention in almost every text (thirteen of the fifteen). But why did a school funding case, which merely reaffirmed the status quo, garner so much attention in the decades since it first arrived at the Court? To answer this question, one first has to understand what *Rodriguez* is really "about." And this is not a simple matter.

Since the controversy in *Rodriguez* involved schools and school districts, the case is obviously about education. But the schools in question were public, not private, and so an additional element is present. If politics is, as Harold Lasswell so famously concluded, about "who gets what, when, and how," then *Rodriguez* — with its focus on the distribution of education as a public good — is about politics. In addition, however, the plaintiffs in this case were all poor, and it was *their* relative and collective poverty, not just an education funding system that relied on local monies to support schools, that resulted in the allegedly inferior schools that provided the reason for the parents' complaint. So this is a case about wealth. Finally, Demetrio Rodriguez and the other plaintiffs were of Mexican descent, and the Edgewood School District in which they resided was essentially (90 to 95 percent) Mexican American. *Rodriguez* is, therefore, also about race.

What stands out about *Rodriguez*, however, is not just that it addresses the subjects of education, politics, wealth, and race, but rather the curious way in which all four of these topics interact within the case. In fact, it is the way that the Supreme Court ultimately understands this relationship that makes *Rodriguez* a landmark case in U.S. law and society.

## Republican Schoolmasters

Education, politics, and wealth have historically shared a relationship. Plato was perhaps the first to explicitly notice this, placing various forms of education at the center of the ideal "city in speech" that he constructed in the *Republic*. The lessons that were to be part of this educational regime were all directed toward unifying the city. At the same time and for a similar reason, Plato suggested that, once again under the best regime, private wealth would have to be severely restricted. Just as education might help to bring the city together, the inequality resulting from private property might tear it in two. About two thousand years later, the British philosopher John Locke, who shared Plato's interest in education, would take a very different tack when it came to wealth, arguing that the *protection* of private property is a core function of any legitimate government (Locke's writings on education show a similar private orientation). In newly independent America, James Madison, the guiding intellectual force behind the U.S. Constitution, borrowed from both thinkers, accepting differences in wealth as one of the major causes of divisive "factions" within a country and designing governmental mechanisms to counter the worst effects of the inevitable divisions.

But in discussing wealth, Madison also offered a lesson on education. In *Federalist Paper 10*, Madison addressed the problem of "faction," which he defined as a group "united and actuated by some common impulse of passion, or of interest, adverse to the rights of other citizens, or to the permanent and aggregate interests of the community." Madison did not counsel the elimination of these self-interested groups. He wrote, "the most common and durable source of factions has been the various and unequal distribution of property," and Madison believed in the sanctity of property rights. The best that could be done, therefore, is to accommodate factions, curbing their dominion.

As Madison wrote about factions in *Federalist Paper 10*, however, his real target lay elsewhere. He was aware that the government he helped to design violated a key element of so-called "republican" political thought. The philosopher Montesquieu, for example, had argued that successful republics had to encompass "only a small territory." Yet the republic formed by the new constitution imagined a "more perfect union" of thirteen loosely connected former colonies into one massive nation. How could such an extensive nation be called a republic?

To understand Madison's implicit response to this question, one first must look at why Montesquieu and others were so enamored with the idea of small republics. In a small country, the argument went, it was easier for each individual to comprehend the relationship between his or her own good and the good of the larger whole. Therefore, it was possible in a small republic to achieve the "self-renunciation" of private interest that was crucial to governing for the common good. Absent a perception of the common good, a republic — from the Latin *res publica*, meaning "affairs of the public" — quite literally could not exist. Of course, individuals are not born with this sense of that which is held in common. Hence the need for education. But such an education could only succeed in a small place, since individuals would have to be able to comprehend the connection between their own welfare and the good of the state. It followed that if Madison could defeat the argument for "republican education," he would at the same time undercut the case against large republics. This is precisely what he attempts in *Federalist Paper 10*.

Apparently Madison agreed with the British philosopher Thomas Hobbes that, if they are at liberty to do so, "masterless men" will seek their own interest. One way to eliminate factions, therefore, was to take away liberty. Although this might work, it would be an "unwise" remedy — a cure that was worse than the disease. The only sensible way to attack the cause of factions, therefore, would be "by giving to every citizen the same opinions, the same passions, and the same interests." The citizens might then use their freedom to pursue public, rather than private, goods. This is only a slightly veiled reference to republican education: education that would result in everyone having "the same interests." Although such education might work in theory, it was, in Madison's word, "impracticable." Why? Because, according to him, the differences that lead to competing interests are "sown in the nature of man." Recall that "the most common and durable source" of factions, according to Madison, was the "unequal distribution of property." So what Madison argued in *Federalist Paper 10* was that rich and poor are unlikely to be educated out of their different interests. Madison then turned republican political thought on its head, advocating large republics as the best means for multiplying and thus diffusing factions. Implicit in Madison's message, however, was the idea that this large republic would not be concerned with educating citizens. Education would be a private matter.

---

## Public Education in America

Although it might be argued that, under the system designed by Madison, education would not be a formal concern of the national government, it remained, for Madison and the other Founding Fathers, a national interest. Benjamin Franklin (who reportedly spent only two years in formal education) wrote: "Nothing can more effectually contribute to the cultivation and improvement of a Country than a proper Education of youth." Madison himself counseled that "only a well-educated people can be permanently a free people." John Adams shared the younger Madison's thoughts, concluding that only a people capable of understanding their rights will act in defense of them. And Madison's closest ally, Thomas Jefferson, is famous for drafting "A Bill for the More General Diffusion of Knowledge," in which he warned of tyranny and wrote that "the most effectual means of preventing this [tyranny] would be, to illuminate, as far as practicable, the minds of the people at large." Jefferson, in fact, went so far as to call for dividing up the counties of Virginia into separate hundreds (districts), building a schoolhouse in each. Three years of education would be provided free of charge, and teachers would be paid in the same manner "as other county expenses," with the inhabitants of the district responsible only for boarding expenses.

Of the Framers mentioned above, however, only Franklin attended the Constitutional Convention of 1787 in Philadelphia with Madison. Unlike the Northwest Ordinance, written in the same year as the Constitution, which explicitly stated that "schools and the means of education shall be forever encouraged," the Constitution was silent on education. So, where the Constitution gave explicit authority to Congress to build "Post Offices and post roads," no parallel power was granted for the construction of public schools. Therefore, if public education was to emerge in the United States, it would have to be instituted by the states, not the federal government. Another way of looking at this omission is to understand that, although the argument in support of public education might be national, control would be exercised by the states. But the handoff of responsibility was not yet complete. State control over education was mostly ceded to smaller subdivisions or townships.

By 1787, many of states had already taken small steps toward instituting some form of public education. Indeed, a majority of the state constitutions drafted immediately after independence called for the support of education, although not overtly for public schools. As one author described these provisions, they were "long, eloquently written, and indefinite." Consequently, they did not provide much direction. As a result, at the dawn of the nineteenth century, most schools were private, although with some public control and acknowledgment in the form of state incorporation.

In response to the leveling forces of Jacksonian democracy, all this began to change. If the United States was to have the type of political equality implicit in Jacksonian rhetoric, some basic education would have to be provided to all, regardless of ability to pay. Moreover, there was a rudimentary sense that political and economic equality were linked, and that the latter would only be possible if the poor had access to education. The argument was well stated by Horace Mann, secretary of the Massachusetts Board of Education and a leading advocate for universal public education. In 1848, Mann wrote that "nothing but universal education can counterwork" what he saw as the "domination of capital and servility of labor. . . . But, if education be equally diffused, it will draw property after it by the strongest of all attractions; for such a thing never did happen, and never can happen, as that an intelligent and practical body of men should be permanently poor."

But Mann and other reformers were not just advocating for economic equality and recognizing the economic benefits of education. Elsewhere, Mann would suggest that children ought to remain in public education until "the state shall have secured to all its children, that basis of knowledge and morality, which is indispensable to its [the state's] own security." Notice how, for Mann, what might be called the "civic" usefulness of education merges with its economic side effects. Wealth, education, and politics are mutually reinforcing. This theme was further developed by the philosopher and educator John Dewey, who added that, through both subject and method, public education might provide crucial support for American democracy.

Once again, however, although the arguments in favor of free public education were national in character, the actual establishment of the public schools began as a local phenomenon. In modern school funding cases, much is made of the notion of "local control" over schools. Indeed, in *San Antonio v. Rodriguez*, the unequal Texas school funding system was ultimately allowed by the Supreme Court based on the justices' acceptance of the importance of local control. It is curious to note, therefore, that local school districts were not the result of a conscious choice by state legislators to empower local communities. Instead, the precedent was set by townships building schools. Writing about American townships in 1835— right about when public education was beginning to establish itself within the states —

Alexis de Tocqueville used the construction of schools as an example of the relationship between state governments and townships, observing that "the existence of a school is imposed, but the township builds it, pays for it, and directs it." Eventually, even smaller school districts were created to accommodate sprawling township populations, and these districts were given responsibility for financing at least some portion of the schools.

As emigration to the United States increased, the need for a common educational experience became more tangible and more controversial. Some who were born in the United States were suspicious of the more recent arrivals. The tension was exacerbated by the fact that many of the new immigrants did not speak English and did not practice the various forms of Protestantism that dominated American religious life.

As has already been explained, private education preceded the public schools. More often than not, private schools were sectarian. As public school systems began to evolve, the democratic quality of those schools — often tellingly referred to as "common" — was emphasized, and private sectarian schools began to be seen as a threat. As early as 1876 the Republican platform asserted that "the public school system of the several states is the bulwark of the American Republic. . . . We recommend an amendment to the Constitution of the United States forbidding the application of any public funds or property for the benefit of any schools or institutions under sectarian control." Although such an amendment never became part of the U.S. Constitution, several states added so-called "Blaine amendments" (named after James Blaine, the congressmember who had first proposed the federal version of the amendment in 1875) to their own constitutions. Other states took this thesis to its logical conclusion and tried to ban private education altogether. In *Pierce v. Society of Sisters* (1925), however, the Supreme Court ruled that such laws violated the Due Process Clause of the Fourteenth Amendment.

What remained, therefore, were several competing ideas about the necessity for free public education. Clearly individuals gained economic benefits from having been educated. Therefore, it made sense for parents to pay local taxes to their local schools. Yet the equality and knowledge that resulted from free public education also contributed to the health of American democracy. Indeed, it was the shared social benefits of education that justified the taxing for educational purposes of those who had no children.

By tradition, school funding throughout the United States (at least for primary and secondary schools) was left in the hands of local school districts, with some help from the states. There was an unintended consequence to this system. The primary method of collecting money for schools was the ad valorem property tax (Latin for "according to value" — the amount of property tax owed varies with the value of the property). Obviously, property-poor districts were unlikely to generate very much money for their schools. Depending upon who was included within a particular school district, that district might be labeled as rich or poor. If there was any correlation at all between the money that a school had and the resulting quality of education, then the funding system was certain to produce inequality. Poor school districts could be expected to produce students less able to attain economic equality and less able to participate fully in democratic government. If one supposed that the school district lines were gerrymandered, then the relationship between wealth, politics, and education was obvious.

---

## Brown v. Board of Education

By 1954, the debate about public education would take an interesting turn as the issue of race moved front and center. Although a free public education was theoretically available to all children by this time, it was, in the South at least, provided on a strictly segregated basis. If public schools served democracy by providing a common and equal experience to children, then black children were being short-changed. The implication of legal segregation of schools was that blacks were not full-fledged members of the democratic polity. Moreover, since black schools were often academically inferior to white schools, black children would have a hard time acquiring the skills they would need to participate in politics, even if that participation was not foreclosed to them by other means (such as poll taxes, literacy tests, and other attempts to keep them from voting), which were common at the time.

The inequality of segregated schools was not really a new issue at all. In the mid-1800s, segregated schools in Boston had been challenged under the Massachusetts Constitution based on the argument that segregated schools perpetuated a "caste" system in which all children were not regarded as full members of society. And in 1899, in the case of *Cummings v. Board of Education*, the U.S. Supreme Court heard a challenge by a group of African American parents in Georgia when the school board cut off funds for a segregated black high school. The Court decided in favor of the school board. Curiously enough, the author of the Court's opinion in *Cummings*, Justice John Marshall Harlan, had three years earlier authored a famous dissent in the case of *Plessy v. Ferguson* (1896). In *Plessy*, the Court upheld a Louisiana law that mandated separate railway cars for black and white riders, stating that facilities could be "separate but equal." Justice Harlan had objected to that decision, arguing that "the Constitution is color-blind" and that the Louisiana statute was based "on the ground that colored citizens are so inferior and degraded that they cannot be allowed to sit in public coaches occupied by white citizens."

Groups such as the National Association for the Advancement of Colored People (NAACP) that wanted to end school segregation knew they could never hope to effect this change through the southern legislatures. Their only hope, therefore, was to go to court. The NAACP knew the argument it made was not only about education; it was about equality. Therefore, the strategy was to bring a case challenging segregation under the Equal Protection Clause of the Fourteenth Amendment. In order to be successful, however, the NAACP would ultimately need to get the Court to reverse *Plessy*. When a young attorney named Thurgood Marshall took over the NAACP Legal Defense and Education Fund, he began to make progress toward bringing such a case.

The work of Marshall and his predecessors at the NAACP culminated in four cases known collectively as *Brown v. Board of Education* (1954). Although *Brown* was first argued before the Court in December of 1952, it was held over for reargument during the October 1953 term, with a request that both sides answer several questions. The first question the justices asked the parties was "What evidence is there that the Congress which submitted and the state legislatures and conventions which ratified the Fourteenth Amendment contemplated or did not contemplate, understood or did not understand, that it would abolish segregation in public schools?" When Chief Justice Earl Warren finally handed down an opinion for the Court in May of 1954, he offered an important answer.

Regardless of the intentions of the Framers of the Fourteenth Amendment or the states that ratified it in 1868, Warren wrote: "Today, education is perhaps the most important function of state and local governments. Compulsory school attendance laws and the great expenditures for education both demonstrate our recognition of the importance of education to our democratic society. It is required in the performance of our most basic public responsibilities, even service in the armed forces. It is the very foundation of good citizenship." This was one of the strongest statements ever made by the Supreme Court about the civic nature of education. It was also a strong argument for equality in educational opportunity.

―――――

## From *Brown* to *Rodriguez*

It is easy to see the potential link between *Brown* and *Rodriguez*. Indeed, as Justice William O. Douglas would later observe, there are even echoes of *Plessy*'s "separate but equal" standard in *Rodriguez*. The Edgewood School District at the center of the dispute was (and still is) essentially a Mexican American school district. Although there was no Texas law that said Mexican Americans could not attend the same schools as white students, school district lines were drawn around existing neighborhoods; since neighborhoods were (effectively though not legally) segregated, so were the schools. If these school districts were unequal, then one might argue that the separation involved was not even cloaked by the (*Plessy*) argument of separate but equal facilities.

*Rodriguez* was, nevertheless, different from *Brown*. In *Brown*, the segregation of students had been *de jure*; that is, "as a matter of law." In *Rodriguez*, any segregation was *de facto*, or, "as a matter of fact." De facto cases have always presented a special challenge to the courts. Indeed, in the years following *Brown*, lower courts struggled to decide whether the full implementation of the Supreme Court's decision in that case demanded the end of de facto as well as de jure segregation. Congress even entered the debate when, in the Civil Rights Act of 1964, it declared that " 'desegregation' shall not mean the assignment of students to public schools in order to overcome racial imbalance."

By the time *Rodriguez* reached the High Court, however, it was fairly clear that a majority of the justices were not inclined to try to remedy cases of de facto segregation, seeing them as distinguishable from the situation argued in *Brown*.

Another obvious difference is that *Brown* addressed discrimination against African Americans, whereas *Rodriguez* was about discrimination against Mexican Americans, which had been practiced in that area since the United States acquired a large portion of Mexico in the nineteenth century.

When the Edgewood School District was first drawn, it contained virtually no Mexican Americans, so it was difficult for the plaintiffs to argue that the district itself was drawn in a discriminatory manner. Gradually, and in a process that became common in the borderlands region as Mexican Americans congregated in certain neighborhoods, whites moved out. This was not purely self-selection. Deed restrictions in many areas prevented houses being sold to Mexican Americans, African Americans, or Native Americans, including those of mixed race. The result was that, where whites could move "up and out" of poor neighborhoods, Mexican Americans had no such freedom. They were all but forced to remained in poor neighborhoods. If there was any correlation between district wealth and the quality of local schools, then Mexican Americans were guaranteed an inferior education.

An inferior education is often associated with both economic and political inequality. This problem was recognized fairly early by the Mexican American community. In 1929, Texan attorney Alonso Perales formed the League of United Latin American Citizens (LULAC) to focus on civil rights concerns including the problem of education. Perales explained that "if we [Latinos] wish to have success in this world individually or collectively, we must accept as our duty the raising of our intellectual norms." In the years prior to the Court's 1954 decision in *Brown*, LULAC was very active in integrating schools, particularly in California; in both 1945 and 1946, LULAC won important cases that led to the end of Mexican American segregation in that state.

In 1948, a second group that would often work with LULAC, the America GI Forum, was founded by Hector Garcia. Garcia, like many of the early leaders of the Mexican American civil rights movement (including Demetrio Rodriguez), was a veteran of World War II. He was disturbed by the many incidents of discrimination that afflicted Mexican American and other Hispanic veterans. The American GI Forum first gained national attention when it worked to resolve what has become known as the "Longoria Incident." When Hispanic war hero Felix Longoria died, his widow was told that he could not be brought to a "whites only" funeral home. Garcia and the American GI Forum worked together with then Senator Lyndon Johnson to remedy this injustice. Eventually, Longoria was buried in Arlington National Cemetery, and the controversy brought national attention to Garcia's group.

Like LULAC, the GI Forum saw that education was crucial to equality. Indeed, the GI Forum motto states that "education is freedom and freedom should be everyone's business." In 1948, the GI Forum joined LULAC in helping to fund the Texas case of *Delgado v. Bastrop Independent School District.* Unlike California, Texas never had an official policy of segregation of Mexican Americans; in the words of Guadalupe San Miguel, Jr., segregation was "not prescribed, but practiced." School officials simply assigned Mexican American children to different, often inferior, schools. In *Delgado*, this practice was challenged by Mexican American parents precisely because segregation was not authorized by the Texas law. The federal district court for the Western District of Texas (the same court that would hear the *Rodriguez* case about twenty years later) ruled in favor of the parents, issuing an injunction against the state that forbade further segregation of students "of Mexican or Latin descent." This decision thus left in place the legal segregation of African Americans, which was explicitly allowed under the Texas Constitution.

According to most scholars of Mexican American school segregation in Texas, *Delgado* and other similar cases had little impact on what was actually happening in the schools. Even in the years following *Brown*, little changed. By 1968, a third Mexican American civil rights organization, the Mexican American Legal Defense and Education Fund (MALDEF), was formed by Pete Tijerina, a lawyer who worked for LULAC. Tijerina was particularly angry about the discrimination against Mexican Americans in the Texas courts. He contacted Jack Greenberg, who by then held Thurgood Marshall's former position as the head of the NAACP Legal and Educational Defense Fund (Marshall had left the NAACP to become Solicitor General and then an Associate Justice on the U.S. Supreme Court). Together, Greenberg and Tijerina worked to secure a grant from the Ford Foundation that funded MALDEF, in the hopes it would do for Mexican Americans what the NAACP had done for African Americans.

## School Funding in Texas

LULAC, MALDEF, and the American GI Forum were all active when *San Antonio v. Rodriguez* was filed in the summer of 1968. Still, there was always a question about whether *Rodriguez* really involved racial discrimination. One might argue that the inequality suffered by the parents who brought *Rodriguez* to court was a function not of segregation but of the Texas school financing system. If so, the inherent discrimination affected all students living in poor districts, not just those of Mexican American descent.

In the development of its public school system, Texas mirrored what had happened or would happen in the rest of the states. In 1839 the Congress of the Republic of Texas parceled off land in each county to be used for public schools. Six years later, when Texas became a state, Article 10, section 1 of its constitution declared: "A general diffusion of knowledge being essential to the preservation of the rights and liberties of the people, it shall be the duty of the legislature of this state to make suitable provision for the support and maintenance of public schools." The legislature was therefore called upon "to establish free schools throughout the state of Texas."

By 1854, school districts were established and the state legislature allocated 2 million dollars to what was called the Permanent School Fund. Under the 1876 constitution, revenue from 52 million acres of state land (including any proceeds from the sale of that land), along with a percentage of the occupational tax and the poll tax, was added to this fund. Then, in 1933, a state-wide ad valorem property tax was added for the support of schools. The revenues from this tax, along with money from the Permanent School Fund, combined to form the Available School Fund. The money from this fund was distributed on a per pupil basis.

The Available School Fund provided only part of the money for the schools. School districts supplemented the monies available from the state fund with revenue gathered from local property taxes. If the property wealth within each of the districts had remained substantially equal, then the result would have been fairly equalized school funding (depending on local tax rates). Writing in 1974, Mark Yudof, a professor at the University of Texas Law School who was involved in the *Rodriguez* case, offered the following summary of a Texas Research Council report that explained what had happened by the early twentieth century:

> Some communities in Texas were more willing than others to bear heavy local property taxes. There were other communities which had such substantial property wealth per pupil that enrichment beyond the state minimum became inevitable — even at marginal local tax rates. Still others were not really communities at all, but only hastily incorporated school districts, levying no taxes and designated as havens for affluent landowners.

In response to these problems and fearing future school population explosions, the Texas legislature in 1947 formed the Gilmer-Aiken Committee to study and recommend changes to the state's school financing system. The Gilmer-Aiken Committee was made up of an equal number of legislators and members drawn from the general public. The committee issued a report with the not-so-prosaic title *To Have What We Must.* In the report, the committee recommended a new system to fund the schools named the Minimum Foundation Program. With the adoption of the committee recommendations, Texas for the first time attempted to adjust for interdistrict disparities. Under the Minimum Foundation Program, the Texas legislature would calculate a basic foundation amount based on what the state thought was necessary to pay teacher salaries and other expenses. The state would then provide enough funds to cover about 80 percent of this foundation amount. The remaining 20 percent, known as the Local Fund Assignment, would be provided by the local school districts. Each local district, however, would not be required to provide an equal share of the Local Fund Assignment. Instead, an economic index was used to calculate the relative wealth of school districts. Poorer districts would be expected to contribute much less of the Local Fund Assignment. The districts remained free, after paying their local share, to raise additional property tax revenues with no reduction in state aid.

By all accounts, the Minimum Foundation Program did improve the situation in Texas. The problem was that the actual foundation amount was the result of what we now call residual budgeting: The state calculated how much money was left after other programs were funded and used this amount to determine what was necessary for a minimally adequate education. Huge disparities in school funding could still exist, since districts did not have an equal ability to raise money beyond that provided by the Minimum Foundation Program. Moreover, since wealthier districts might also have better qualified teachers, they would be eligible for more state funding.

By 1965, the problems with the Minimum Foundation Program had become obvious, and the governor at the time, John Connally, tried to address them by creating the Governor's Committee on Public School Education. The resulting report, *The Challenge and the Chance*, made some bold recommendations including the consolidation of smaller districts and reform of the economic index. Most of the recommendations, however, were ignored by the legislature. Therefore, the Minimum Foundation Program was essentially still in place in 1968 when Demetrio Rodriguez and the other Mexican American parents went to court.

What drove Mr. Rodriguez and his fellow plaintiffs to court? Certainly one could speculate that the rise of Mexican American civil rights organizations, along with the failure of Texas to adopt new school funding reforms, might have precipitated a suit over school financing by Mexican American parents. Moreover, similar school funding cases had arisen in other states. As the reader shall see in the next chapter, however, the case of *San Antonio v. Rodriguez* was not, strictly speaking, the result of any of these events. In fact, one might argue that the *Rodriguez* case moved forward in spite of them.

# CHAPTER 2

# Beginnings

How did the case of *San Antonio Independent School District v. Rodriguez* actually begin? When describing a significant historical event, it is tempting to look for causation; to say that "A led to B, which then resulted in C." The problem, however, is that history is rarely so linear. More often than not, several loosely related events or actions occur at approximately the same time, and an almost Jungian synchronicity allows the events to cross-pollinate. This is what happened in the case of *Rodriguez*. Therefore, the best approach is to work backward from the Supreme Court decision, tracing the various actions to when they were first initiated.

This is what the journalist William Greider attempted to do in a piece that appeared in the same March 22, 1973, edition of the *Washington Post* that carried the headline "Property Tax Use on Schools Upheld." Greider knew that in the case of *Serrano v. Priest* (1971), the California Supreme Court had declared that state's school financing system to be inconsistent with the demands of both the federal and state constitutions. According to the California justices, this dual constitutional infirmity was the direct result of California making "the quality of a child's education depend upon the resources of his school district and ultimately upon the pocketbook of his parents." Since this was nearly identical to the issue raised in *Rodriguez*, it made sense for Greider to search for a precedent in the former. This led him to an individual who played a critical role in all of the early school funding litigation: John E. Coons, who was at the time a law professor at the University at California at Berkeley.

Coons's interest in school finance had begun about a decade earlier while he was teaching at the Northwestern University School of Law in Chicago. In 1961, Coons had been hired by the U.S. Commission on Civil Rights to conduct a study on desegregation in the

Chicago schools. What caught the young law professor's eye was a form of inequality that had not been addressed in the early desegregation cases. In looking at how schools were financed, Coons noticed that property-rich districts had enormous advantages when it came to raising funds for local schools. A rich district could tax its property at a low rate and still have much more money to spend on local schools than a poor district with very high property taxes. Therefore, whether a student attended a well-funded school was to a large degree dependent on the property wealth of the district in which he or she resided. This was a form of inequality, he thought, that might have constitutional significance.

A few years later, Coons began working on this problem with two of his law students, Stephen Sugarman and William Clune. By 1969, these three had published an article and a year later a book, *Private Wealth and Public Education*, examining how schools were funded. They recommended a more rational system and suggested a possible litigation strategy through which reform might be achieved. For anyone interested in bringing a school finance case, the Coons team (as they became known) offered a legal brief backed by data in the form of their book.

John Coons and his students, however, were not alone in criticizing school financing schemes or in offering book-length arguments in favor of their positions. In 1968, for example, Arthur Wise published a book based on his doctoral dissertation in which he argued that the Equal Protection Clause of the Fourteenth Amendment mandated "equal dollars per pupil" as a funding principle. His theory was based on the "one person, one vote" standard articulated by the Supreme Court in the reapportionment cases. Wise thought that the voting rights mantra should be transformed to read "one dollar, one scholar." At the same time, others were asserting that equalized funding was not sufficient; that students with greater needs ought to have greater resources. The Coons team, however, took a different tack. As they wrote: "requiring equality of expenditures per pupil statewide might be a catchy device for terminating the existing injustices; it might also be an effective way to terminate public education." Theirs was a more modest proposal.

Known by the seemingly interchangeable titles of "power equalizing," "fiscal neutrality," or "Proposition I," the Coons, Sugarman, and Clune formula was straightforward: school districts willing to tax themselves at an equal rate ought to be able to raise an equal amount of money. Then, as now, variations in property wealth from district to district meant that this would not happen without state intervention. Here is how they described the problem in their 1970 book: "Imagine a state divided into two school districts, A and B, each with 100 pupils. District A has a total wealth of $10,000 ($100 per pupil). District B has a total of $90,000, or $900 per pupil. Each decides to tax itself at the rate of 10 percent for schools, yielding respectively $10 and $90 per pupil." Under the theory of power equalizing, the state would make up the $80 difference between what the poor and rich districts could raise using this equal tax rate. In this way, with the help of the state, an equal tax "effort" would result in an equal monetary yield, regardless of the property wealth of a district.

The Coons team's work became well known within the larger legal community, particularly among those seeking to use the law and courts to remedy what they thought were social injustices and to help those who were living in poverty. This was precisely the aim of the newly formed Western Center on Law and Poverty. Derrick Bell, who was one of the center's first executive directors, was familiar with the Coons team's formula. One evening in 1968, Bell and his colleague Charles Jones happened to be at a party with John Serrano, a psychiatric social worker who lived in East Los Angeles. The three began talking, and the subject turned to a discussion of schools, specifically the condition of many of the schools in the poorer sections of California. About a year earlier, the principal of the East Los Angeles school that Serrano's two sons had attended recommended that he move the bright young boys to a better school. Serrano was upset with the principal's implicit acceptance of the inadequate conditions at his East Los Angeles school. Eventually, this conversation would result in the name Serrano being forever linked with the legal battle over school finance. His son would become the lead plaintiff in *Serrano v. Priest* (1971), a class action case brought on behalf of students in poor school districts throughout California.

Although John Coons would later refer to *Serrano* as "part of a rash of ill-conceived litigation," the Coons team would play a central role in that case. Indeed, two members of the group, Coons and Steven Sugarman, joined the argument before the California Supreme Court. And when *Serrano* was decided in the plaintiff's favor, the California Supreme Court's opinion was sprinkled with references to Coons's work and the power equalizing formula that the group had championed.

Although power equalizing was not formally endorsed by the California Supreme Court in *Serrano*, it is easy to understand why it was important to the resulting decision. Prior to *Serrano* — as part of the "rash" of litigation — two other school finance cases had already been dismissed by federal courts in decisions that were summarily affirmed by the U.S. Supreme Court. In *McInnis v. Shapiro*, handed down on November 15, 1968, a federal district court in Illinois ruled against a group of Cook County students who had argued that the Illinois school funding system violated the Equal Protection Clause of the Fourteenth Amendment. Then, in May of 1969, the U.S. District Court for the Western District of Virginia ruled against a similar Fourteenth Amendment claim in *Burruss v. Wilkerson*. In each of these cases the district courts cited the lack of judicially manageable standards for restructuring a state's school funding system as a reason for rejecting the plaintiffs' claims.

Coons's model of power equalizing was important because it provided the manageable standard that had heretofore been absent. States could retain their basic funding systems but they would have to guarantee equal yield for equal effort. By 1976, when the *Serrano* case came back to the California Supreme Court (*Serrano II*), the justices gave more explicit support to power equalizing, and, for a brief time, the California legislature wrote power equalizing into their school finance law.

With one ultimately significant exception — the reliance on state constitutional provisions — the legal argument in *Serrano* matched the claims made on behalf of the Edgewood parents in *Rodriguez*. Although it is natural to assume the California case set a precedent for the Texas case, this is not what happened. Although the first *Serrano* decision was handed down on August 30, 1971, a full year-and-a-half before the U.S. Supreme Court handed down its decision in *Rodriguez*, the Texas case was actually filed in July of 1968, three years before the California Supreme Court issued its historic ruling. Indeed, there is some indication that John Coons and his colleagues did not even want *Rodriguez* to come to court. More importantly, there is no evidence that Arthur Gochman, the attorney for the plaintiffs in *Rodriguez*, even knew about the Coons team's work when he filed his case. Indeed, his initial briefs failed to mention either *Serrano* or the work of Coons, Sugarman, and Clune. In fact, when the *Serrano* decision came down and reporters began calling Gochman asking him to comment on the California case, his initial reaction was to say that he really didn't know anything more about the California case other than what he had read in the newspaper.

---

## The Edgewood District Concerned Parents Association

If one were going to select a date upon which *Rodriguez* can be said to have "begun" it probably should be May 16, 1968, about two years before the publication of the Coons team's *Private Wealth and Public Education*. On that date, about 400 students at Edgewood High School decided to stage a walk-out. They had several grievances. Many of the students' friends had been drafted into the war in Vietnam; some never to return. Regardless of their feelings about the war, the sacrifice that graduates of Edgewood High School had made for their country led to questions about reciprocity. At the very least, the students thought that they deserved better school facilities. As Demetrio Rodriguez, the lead plaintiff in the case, would later describe it, the problems ranged "from Bunsen burners to broken windows." The school had few supplies, no air conditioning, and the school buildings were crumbling. There were even health concerns since at least one floor of the school was known to be infested with bats. Moreover, too many of the teachers were not fully certified.

Arguably, the most significant result of the walk-out was not its impact on the school district's administrators, but rather its effect on the parents of the students. In the wake of the walk-out, the parents began to talk to one another about the problems in the schools. Several of the parents had been active in political movements, and they knew that they would have to organize if they hoped to change the situation. They quickly formed the Edgewood District Concerned Parents Association. The group was led by a woman named Alberta Snid, a widowed mother of four. Among the parents who were charter members was a man named Demetrio Rodriguez, a sheet metal worker employed at a local air force base. A Navy and Air Force veteran who had served in both World War II and the Korean War, Rodriguez had long been involved with Mexican American civil rights organizations. He was a member of both the American GI Forum and League of United Latin American Citizens (LULAC), and had, in the aftermath of *Brown v. Board of Education* (1954), traveled to other parts of Texas in support of desegregation efforts.

Rodriguez and the other members of the parents group knew very little about school finance. The entire terminology was foreign to them. They were aware, however, that they had overwhelmingly supported spending on their schools when such issues were put before them on the ballot. As a result of this, the Edgewood School District had one of the highest tax rates in the area. Yet despite this high level of support, the parents knew that their schools were not in the same condition as those in other parts of San Antonio. The parents put these facts together and arrived at a logical conclusion: someone, perhaps a member of the local school board, was receiving bribes or kickbacks, or was in some other way stealing the money. That must be why, they thought, there was no money left to pay teachers and repair schools. Theft, of course, was a violation of the law. They would need to contact a lawyer.

A young man named Willie Velasquez had met several times with the Edgewood parents. Velasquez, who would go on to found the Southwest Voter Registration Project and be awarded a posthumous Presidential Medal of Freedom for his work, was active in Mexican American political and labor movements. When he learned that the group needed an attorney, he suggested Arthur Gochman. Earlier, Velasquez had organized the farm and cannery workers in Crystal City, Texas. They had temporarily taken over city hall, and this had allowed Velasquez to meet Gochman, who was then a volunteer city attorney. Although Gochman and Velasquez had never worked together, they had supported the same causes.

The Edgewood parents decided to follow Velasquez's advice and had the leader of their group, Alberta Snid, contact Arthur Gochman's office to set up an appointment. When Snid and some of the other parents arrived at Gochman's office in the Frost Bank building in downtown San Antonio, they explained the situation to him. Gochman agreed to look into the matter.

After he found out who was serving on the Edgewood School Board, Gochman quickly concluded that no crime was being committed, at least not in the traditional sense of that term. He knew and respected many of the members of the board, and the ones he did not know had fine reputations. It appeared unlikely, therefore, that any-one was stealing any money. Indeed, there was very little money to steal. The Edgewood Independent School District did contain some valuable property, particularly Kelly Air Force Base, where Demetrio Rodriguez worked. But Air Force bases do not pay local property taxes, and the remaining property tax base in the Edgewood district was very small, with only about 10 percent being valued at more than $10,000. Another problem was the abysmal rate of tax collection. Ironically, state laws prohibited the district from spending on legal fees more than 15 percent of the value of the tax that might be recovered by a lawsuit. So the low property values also limited the resources available for remedying the inequality.

The result was that no matter how willing the Edgewood parents were to support taxes, not very much money would be raised for the schools. Although Edgewood had the highest property tax rate in the San Antonio area, the district had only been able to raise about $26 per student. In the nearby community of Alamo Heights, a much lower tax rate yielded $333 per student. Although the state foundation program and federal funds reduced the disparity in per pupil spending, a gap of almost $250 per student remained.

As Gochman looked at this data, a natural question arose: Although this funding inequality might appear unjust, was it illegal? The young lawyer looked for legal precedents that might support a claim that poor funding amounted to a form of discrimination. *Serrano* was not available since it had not yet been handed down. While doing his legal research, however, Gochman had come across a decision written by Judge J. Skelly Wright in a case out of the District of Columbia. The case, *Hobson v. Hansen* (1967), in many ways involved issues similar to those in San Antonio. Here, Gochman thought, was a precedent upon which the Edgewood parents might be able to rely.

––––––

## Precedents to *Hobson v. Hansen*

On May 17, 1954, the Supreme Court had issued its famous decision in the school desegregation case known as *Brown v. Board of Education*. Although the *Brown* case actually involved the Board of Education in Topeka, Kansas, it was one of four cases that the Court decided together in a single, unanimous opinion. This made sense, because all four cases involved exactly the same issue: whether state-sponsored segregated education violated the Equal Protection Clause of the Fourteenth Amendment.

If one were to open the volume of U.S. Reports that contains *Brown*, one would find an additional case, *Bolling v. Sharpe* (1954), which also dealt with racially segregated education. What distinguished *Bolling* from *Brown* was that the former case arose in the District of Columbia.

School segregation in the nation's capital was as old as the District of Columbia public school system itself. In 1805, when that system was first established, black children were left out of the plan. After 1862, when public education was finally offered to African Americans, the plan provided for separate schools. Washington, D.C., was eventually divided up into two "divisions"; Division I for white students and Division II for African Americans. This was the system of school segregation in place in 1950 when Spottswood T. Bolling and several other black students in Washington, D.C., brought a suit against C. Melvin Sharpe, then president of the District of Columbia Board of Education.

Unlike Topeka, Kansas, and the other political subdivisions involved in the *Brown* litigation, the District of Columbia was not, of course, a state. This was a constitutionally significant fact because the Equal Protection Clause of the Fourteenth Amendment, upon which *Brown* was based, says only that *states* may not deny individuals the equal protection of the law. Technically, therefore, it was impossible for the District of Columbia to be found in violation of the Equal Protection Clause. Nevertheless, it was clear to the Supreme Court justices that they could not declare state segregation unconstitutional but at the same time allow essentially federally sponsored segregation to remain intact in the District of Columbia. In a brief six-paragraph opinion, the Court in *Bolling* avoided the problem by discovering an equal protection "component" in the Due Process Clause of the Fifth Amendment. Unlike the Fourteenth, the Fifth Amendment clearly applies to the federal government. Ultimately, the federal government is responsible for the District of Columbia. Therefore, in allowing segregation to take place, the federal government was found to have violated the equal protection component of the Due Process Clause of the Fifth Amendment.

Unlike what had happened in most of the southern states in the aftermath of *Brown*, desegregation in the nation's capital had gone forward rather smoothly. By 1955 the District of Columbia Board of Education had put into place a "neighborhood schools" plan. The idea was that students of all races would simply attend the schools that were closest to their homes. Of course, if neighborhoods were effectively segregated (as they were), then so would be the schools. It was unclear, however, whether *Bolling* (and *Brown*) forbade this type of segregation. Clearly de jure segregation would no longer be allowed, but should de facto segregation be cured?

By the mid-1960s, the neighborhood schools plan, combined with the existence of "optional districts" (within which students had the option to choose the school they would attend) resulted in a highly segregated school system. In fact, not only were the students segregated, but so were the teachers. In many of the schools, the entire faculty was either all black or all white. And the all-white schools were spending about 30 percent more per student than the all-black schools. The inequality was made worse by a "tracking" system under which students were placed on separate curricular paths based on their perceived academic potential. There was a strong correlation between socioeconomic status and academic track; there was also a strong relationship between race and socioeconomic status.

In the mid-1960s, Julius Hobson, a black social activist in Washington, D.C., who had a child in the District of Columbia schools, brought a lawsuit against Carl Hansen, then superintendent of the district's school system. Hobson's argument was complex and involved many interrelated issues. Basically, however, he maintained that the discrimination forbidden under *Bolling* was still taking place.

Although the trial in *Hobson v. Hansen* took place in the federal district court for the District of Columbia, Judge J. Skelly Wright, a judge who sat on the court of appeals for that circuit, presided over the case. Wright had been assigned to the case because district court judges appointed the members of the District of Columbia Board of Education. They were, therefore, indirectly involved in the case. In fact, one of the initial issues addressed in *Hobson* was whether this method of appointment was constitutional. The plaintiffs in *Hobson* had come to court armed with mountains of data and tables supporting their claim. The numbers more than proved the plaintiffs' claims that the District of Columbia schools were almost totally segregated and that the predominantly white schools were better funded. Quite a bit of these data would find their way into Wright's 100-page-plus opinion.

Judge Wright ruled in favor of the plaintiff, Hobson, issuing an injunction that barred the District of Columbia from engaging in either racial or economic discrimination and ordering the district to integrate its schools and to dismantle both the track system and the optional district provision that had exacerbated segregation. Gochman was interested in Wright's opinion because of the way in which the judge had combined the notions of racial and economic discrimination. Wright wrote that "if whites and Negroes, or rich and poor, are to be consigned to separate schools . . . the minimum the Constitution will require and guarantee is that for their objectively measurable aspects these schools be run on the basis of real equality, at least unless any inequalities are adequately justified."

In *Hobson*, therefore, differences in school funding were relevant because of the way in which they corresponded to racial segregation. Recall that the parents who brought their complaints to Arthur Gochman were from a part of San Antonio that was overwhelmingly Mexican American. Gochman concluded that if race and wealth had formed an important nexus in *Hobson*, then perhaps that same nexus could be relied upon by the Edgewood parents.

The Edgewood parents had very little money with which to pay a private attorney like Gochman. Also, he thought this matter ought to be handled by a group that specialized in racial discrimination cases. Gochman decided to draft a legal memorandum detailing the complaints of the Edgewood parents. He sent it, along with a copy of *Hobson*, to the newly formed Mexican American Legal and Education Fund (MALDEF). He expected at least a call back from this organization. Instead, he received a letter informing him that MALDEF was not interested. They had already tried to litigate the issue of racial discrimination in the San Antonio schools before the federal court in Texas. Their cases had been summarily dismissed. If they were to bring any more cases it would have to be in state court using the state constitution. *Hobson*, however, was grounded in the Fourteenth Amendment.

Gochman disagreed with MALDEF's assessment and was unwilling to drop the matter. He scheduled another meeting with the Edgewood parents. At this meeting, he informed the parents that he had decided to take their case and asked them to sign the necessary documents to be filed with the court. Since Alberta Snid was the leader of the group, it would have been logical to make her the lead plaintiff. But this case had racial overtones that might prove important, and her name did not sound Mexican American. "Demetrio Rodriguez," however, was perfect. Perhaps he should sign first. Rodriguez, however, was concerned. "How much will this cost?" he asked the lawyer. When Gochman informed him that he would take the case pro bono (or for free), Rodriguez had only one more question: "Where," he asked, "do I sign?"

In January of 1969, *Hobson* was upheld by the Court of Appeals for the District of Columbia. The decision, however was not unanimous. Among the dissenters was Judge Warren E. Burger. To support his disagreement with the majority, Burger relied on the following quote from a *Harvard Law Review* note: "The *Hobson* doctrine can be criticized for its unclear basis in precedent, its potentially enormous scope, and its imposition of responsibilities which may strain the resources and endanger the prestige of the judiciary." Five months later, Burger would be sworn in as the new Chief Justice of the U.S. Supreme Court. Had Gochman known this he might not have been so willing to bring *Rodriguez* to federal court. As it was, however, he thought that he might have the law on his side. It was politics, however, that he failed to take fully into account. Rarely, however, is the former completely divorced from the latter. Indeed, even the legal arguments upon which Gochman would rely as he litigated the case emanated as much from politics as from the U.S. Constitution.

# CHAPTER 3

# Law and Politics

Courts are influenced by politics. The political branches of government — the Senate and especially the president — seek to influence the behavior of the third branch of government by selecting and confirming ideologically compatible nominees to serve on the bench. If they are successful, the outcome of cases will be affected.

This is a fairly obvious point to make in the early twenty-first century United States, when the appointment of judges at all levels of the system has become an intensely political drama. But this is really nothing new. In 1800, for example, as his single term in office came to an end, President John Adams made sure that his secretary of state, fellow Federalist John Marshall, replaced the aging and sickly Oliver Ellsworth as chief justice of the Supreme Court. This ensured that Adams's successor as president, Thomas Jefferson, would not be able to place a judge who shared the Virginian's fondness for state power in charge of the new nation's highest court. Indeed, this and other partisan appointments to the federal courts, combined with the Federalists' loss of the presidency and Congress in the aftermath of the election of 1800, led Jefferson to conclude that Adams's political party had "retired into the judiciary." And the impact was obvious. For although the Federalists would essentially dissolve as a political party over the next decade, its members' vision for America ultimately triumphed.

Most who followed Adams into the White House would behave in a similar manner, backed by a similar understanding. Richard Nixon, who was first elected to the presidency in 1968, was no exception. In that same year, prior to the November elections, the sitting chief justice, Earl Warren, announced that he was leaving the Court. The incumbent president, Lyndon Johnson, nominated his friend and confidant, Associate Justice Abe Fortas, to fill Warren's spot as chief justice. Fortas's nomination ran into trouble, however, when it was discovered that he had accepted a substantial fee to teach a class at American University. For the first time in history, the Senate filibustered a nomination to the Supreme Court. Eventually, President Johnson withdrew the nomination.

But the story does not end there. Less than a year later, faced with another ethical charge against him, Justice Fortas resigned from the Court. This meant that the newly elected Richard Nixon, who had defeated Johnson's vice president, Hubert Humphrey when Johnson chose not to run for reelection, was quickly presented with the opportunity to fill two vacancies on the Court. Nixon nominated Warren Burger of Minnesota, a staunch advocate for judicial restraint, who was at the time a judge on the Court of Appeals for the District of Columbia circuit, to replace Earl Warren as the Court's leader. The position opened by Fortas's resignation was more of a problem. Two of President Nixon's nominees, Clement Haynsworth of South Carolina and G. Harold Carswell of Florida, failed to gain Senate confirmation. Finally, Nixon managed to get Senate approval for Burger's friend and fellow Minnesotan, Harry Blackmun.

By the time Nixon faced reelection in 1972, two additional Nixon nominees had joined Burger and Blackmun. William Rehnquist, assistant attorney general in the Nixon administration, replaced Justice John Marshall Harlan. A former president of the American Bar Association and successful Richmond attorney, Lewis Powell, was tapped to fill the venerable shoes of Justice Hugo L. Black. Eventually, all of Nixon's nominees would vote to uphold the Texas school finance system, with Justice Powell drafting the majority opinion. Since the final vote in *Rodriguez* was only 5 to 4 in favor of Texas, this was significant.

If Demetrio Rodriguez's defeat was the result of politics, so might have been his victory. The legal framework that was most likely to lead to a successful appeal was itself the result of — or at least set in motion by — a presidential election that took place more than thirty years earlier. Indeed, one of the reasons *San Antonio v. Rodriguez* occupies such an important place in U.S. jurisprudence is that Justice Powell's opinion in *Rodriguez* helped to construct boundaries regarding the Fourteenth Amendment that remain in place to this day. Any contemporary case invoking what has become known as the "two-tier approach" to Equal Protection analysis must work within the confines of the majority opinion in *Rodriguez*. Nevertheless, this same method of analysis might, with the switch of just one vote on the Court, have led to a very different result. Either way, it was this legal approach or "test" that would determine the outcome of the case. So, depending upon how one looks at it, *Rodriguez* fell either in the middle or at the end of a much older legal story with its own political precedents that extended back more than thirty years.

-------

## Footnote 4

When Franklin Delano Roosevelt was first elected president in 1932, the Great Depression was in full swing. In his first inaugural address, FDR observed: "This Nation asks for action, and action now." This statement was not just rhetoric. Within his first 100 days in office, Roosevelt signed more than a dozen bills into law, including the Agricultural Adjustment Act (AAA), which attempted to regulate farm production through the provision of subsidies, and the National Recovery Act (NRA), which allowed the president to impose "codes of fair competition." As a matter of policy, much of this legislation was fairly radical for the time, authorizing the federal government to regulate economic activity in a way that surpassed anything done by prior administrations. But would the legislation be considered constitutional by the Supreme Court? Roosevelt had anticipated this question. In addition to calling for action during his inaugural address, Roosevelt spoke to and dismissed the constitutional concerns obvious in such a challenge to traditional federalism. "Our Constitution," the newly elected president explained, "is so simple and practical that it is possible always to meet extraordinary needs by changes in emphasis and arrangement without loss of essential form."

The Supreme Court quickly disagreed. In the years following FDR's first inauguration, the Court would declare that most of the economic regulations proposed by Roosevelt and New Deal Congress went beyond the powers authorized by the Constitution. The president, however, was not one to suffer defeat quietly. In response to these decisions, Roosevelt went on the offensive against the Court. Following his overwhelming victory in the 1936 presidential election, he proposed what has become known as the "Court-Packing Plan of 1937." Roosevelt's plan would have created a new vacancy on the federal bench for any judge or justice who chose to remain on a court past his seventieth birthday.

Although the court-packing plan applied to all levels of the federal judiciary, its potential impact on the Supreme Court drew the most attention. In 1936, a book about the Court entitled *The Nine Old Men* was published. At that time, six of the nine justices were over seventy. The court-packing plan would have expanded the Court to fifteen members, provided Roosevelt with six new vacancies to fill, and resulted in a clear Roosevelt majority on the Court.

Whether the plan would have ever been approved by Congress is open to debate. While the bill was being considered, however, the primary incentive for passage — the Supreme Court's willingness to challenge the constitutionality of the New Deal — vanished. By mid-1937, the Court had clearly changed its collective mind (this was accomplished by Justice Owen Roberts switching his vote), at least when it came to evaluating Congress's power to pass economic and business regulations. From then on, the presumption was that such legislation was compatible with the limited powers laid out for Congress in Article I, section 8 of the Constitution.

Questions remained, however, about how the Court would approach both state and federal cases that involved noneconomic liberties. These doubts began to be addressed in 1938 in the case of *United States v. Carolene Products*. Justice Harlan F. Stone's majority opinion in that case had far-reaching effects, eventually forming the guidelines for the Court's decision thirty-five years later in *Rodriguez*.

To be accurate, it was not the actual decision in *Carolene Products* that would help to decide *Rodriguez;* rather, it was a famous footnote — Footnote 4— appended to that decision. In a 1982 speech, Justice Powell, who had authored Rodriguez, referred to Footnote 4 of *Carolene Products* as "perhaps the most celebrated footnote in constitutional law." This is because the analysis put forward in Footnote 4 led to what is called the two-tiered model of equal protection analysis that remains at the core of U.S. jurisprudence today.

*United States v. Carolene Products* involved the constitutionality of a statute that prohibited the shipment of milk in which some of the fat had been replaced ("filled milk," as it was called), in interstate commerce. This was the sort of run-of-the-mill business regulation that nowadays would scarcely raise an eyebrow on any court. Prior to 1937, however, such statutes were always open to question. For example, the Court might have asked if Congress was really trying to subsidize dairy farmers under the guise of regulating interstate commerce. In so doing, Congress would have arguably been acting beyond any authority granted to them by the Constitution. Indeed, based on pre-1937 Supreme Court precedents, the trial court in *Carolene Products* had found the act unconstitutional. By the time the case was decided by the Supreme Court, however, careful scrutiny of congressional actions under the Commerce Clause had been abandoned. And so the Court had no trouble overturning the lower court and approving the statute.

Footnote 4 to the majority opinion in *Carolene Products* is several paragraphs long. Each paragraph identifies a specific area of legislation that might not enjoy the presumption of constitutionality granted to business regulations such as the one reviewed in *Carolene Products*. Mentioned were laws that restricted the political processes, disproportionately affected "discrete and insular minorities," or defied a specific prohibition contained within the first ten amendments to the Constitution, including those that had been "incorporated" through the Fourteenth Amendment to apply to the states. Eventually, Footnote 4 would evolve into the two-tier approach to the Equal Protection Clause.

## The Two-Tier Approach

Under the two-tier approach, the Court applies either the strict scrutiny or the rational basis test to legislation challenged under the Equal Protection Clause. In practice, strict scrutiny places the burden of proof on the government in certain cases where there has been an alleged violation of the Equal Protection Clause. The result is that the government must go to great, usually insurmountable, lengths to demonstrate that it has not violated the Constitution. When the Court uses strict scrutiny, it asks whether the ends pursued by the state are "compelling." Of course, whether the goals are judged to be compelling is somewhat subjective on the part of the Court as it examines reasoning in prior opinions. In the decisions issued in the years preceding *Rodriguez*, however, it was difficult to find cases in which the Court had recognized any interests as being "compelling." In *Roe v.*

*Wade*, another controversial case decided by the Court in 1973, Justice Blackmun's opinion did identify the state's interest in the health of a pregnant woman during the second three months (trimester) of her pregnancy, and of her child during the final three months, as compelling. But *Roe* was (and remains) a clear exception to the general rule.

Moreover, under the strict scrutiny standard, even if a state was able to demonstrate a compelling interest, the action undertaken might still be found unconstitutional. For the government was also required to show that the means chosen were the most "necessary," "narrowly tailored," or the "least restrictive" available to reach its compelling ends. These standards required that the government prove its discriminatory action to be absolutely necessary to the goal of the legislation. In other words, this was the only way that the government could accomplish an end that had already been defined as "compelling." It is easy to see why the strict scrutiny standard is so often "fatal in fact." Its requirements are nearly impossible to fulfill.

All of this is in contrast to the second tier of means/ends scrutiny, known as the rational basis standard. When the Court applies this test, it asks only that the ends or interests pursued by a government policy or action be "legitimate." Over the years, this has proven to be a rather forgiving standard, particularly since after 1937 the Court was reluctant to limit the scope of state interests defined as legitimate. Although the Court still examines the means selected by the government in order to advance its ends, under the rational basis standard all it requires is that the means used are "rationally related" to a legitimate government interest. This is a test that is usually hard to fail.

Together, the strict scrutiny and rational basis tests form the two tiers of scrutiny available to those, like the plaintiffs in *Rodriguez*, who would bring challenges under the Equal Protection Clause of the Fourteenth Amendment. The two-tier approach also governs some decisions under the Fifth Amendment since — following its decision in *Bolling v. Sharpe* (1954) — the Supreme Court has recognized an equal protection component within the Due Process Clause of that amendment.

Given the very different requirements of these two standards, one might logically and usually correctly predict the outcome of a case based upon which of the two tiers of review was selected by the Court. Therefore, the two-tiered standard was something of a double-edged sword for litigants raising equal protection challenges. On the one hand, if it could be shown that the action taken by the government was within the category of activities historically subject to the strict scrutiny test, success was virtually guaranteed. On the other hand, if the government could convince the Court that the actions it performed ought only be reviewed under the more lenient rational basis standard, a loss was just as certain.

----

## The Warren Court and the Equal Protection Clause

Two-tiered review did not immediately evolve from Footnote 4. Indeed, in a memo Justice Potter Stewart sent to Justice Powell while Powell was working on his opinion in *Rodriguez*, he insisted that what he called the "compelling state interest doctrine" came from Chief Justice Warren's opinion in *Kramer v. Union School District*, a case that had been decided in 1969. Stewart of course knew that the roots of the test extended back much further. Nevertheless, it had only recently been clearly articulated, and most of the growth in the doctrine could fairly be attributed to the Warren Court. Therefore, it remained an open question whether the Burger Court would continue down the same path. And indeed there was some evidence that this would not be the case.

Writing in the *Harvard Law Review* in the fall of 1972, as *Rodriguez* was before the Court, Professor Gerald Gunther observed that, under the direction of the new chief justice, there was "mounting discontent with the rigid two-tier formulations of the Warren Court's equal protection doctrine." In fact, during the October 1971 Supreme Court term, both Powell and Justice Marshall had authored opinions in which they suggested approaches to equal protection cases that would have moved beyond the traditional two-tier standard. But it was not just the rigid all-or-nothing quality of the two-tier standard that had caused difficulties for the Court.

Historically, there were only two scenarios under which strict scrutiny would be invoked, both of which can be traced back to Footnote 4. First of all, Footnote 4 discussed added protection against violations of the Bill of Rights. Over time this evolved into a more general approach of using strict scrutiny whenever the Court found that a "fundamental right," enumerated or unenumerated in the Bill of Rights, had been infringed upon. Second, the footnote had suggested that this same heightened protection be afforded in cases where a "discrete and insular minority" faced unequal treatment. Such classifications were later referred to as "suspect," and included only those based on race, religion, or national origin.

In addition to cementing in place the stark contrast between strict scrutiny and rational basis, the Warren Court had begun to extend the notion of fundamental rights (or interests) protected by the Equal Protection Clause, and had hinted at the inclusion of new groups into the "suspect classification" category. For example, by the time *Rodriguez* appeared on the Court's docket, the Justices had deemed "fundamental" the right to an appeal in criminal cases, the right to vote, and the right to travel from state to state. In the above-mentioned memo from Potter Stewart to Lewis Powell, Stewart clearly saw a danger in this trend. He wrote: "There is hardly a statute on the books that does not result in treating some people differently than others. There is hardly a statute on the books, therefore, that an ingenious lawyer cannot attack under the Equal Protection Clause. If he can persuade a court that a 'fundamental interest' is involved, then the state cannot possibly meet its resulting burden."

In addition to expanding the category of rights or interests deemed fundamental under the Constitution, the Warren Court had also attempted to broaden the definition of suspect classifications. For example, Justice William Douglas, writing for the Court in the 1966 case of *Harper v. Virginia Board of Elections*, suggested that "lines drawn on the basis of wealth or poverty, like those of race, are traditionally disfavored (citations omitted)." Toward the end of his tenure as chief justice, Earl Warren had relied on *Harper* when he concluded in *McDonald v. Board of Election Commissioners of Chicago* (1969) that classifications based on wealth or race were "highly suspect." Hence there was clearly movement toward expanding the traditional categories of suspect classifications to include those based on wealth.

Litigants who sought to challenge government actions in many different areas were heartened and encouraged by the Warren Court's willingness to stretch the boundaries. In fact, the school finance litigation strategy designed by the Coons team depended on this flexibility. In *Serrano v. Priest* the California Supreme Court had cooperated and applied strict scrutiny, recognizing not only that education was a fundamental interest, but that wealth-based discrimination was a suspect classification.

The Supreme Court, however, had not yet applied these broader standards to school finance when Arthur Gochman filed the Edgewood parents' case in the summer of 1968. Nevertheless, Gochman had Judge Skelly Wright's opinion in *Hobson v. Hansen* (1967) on his side, and he thought that he could rely on the Court to provide a broad reading to the tests required under the Equal Protection Clause. Although Chief Justice Warren had just announced his resignation, Abe Fortas, who had been nominated to replace him at the head of the Court, rarely dissented from the Court's more expansive holdings. Indeed, Gochman thought at the time that he "had a cinch, 6–3."

# Arthur Gochman Goes to Court

## Initial Maneuvers

On June 30, 1968, Arthur Gochman filed his case in the federal district court for the Western District of Texas. The complaint asked that the sections of the Texas Constitution and the Texas Civil Statutes dealing with the funding of public education "be declared unconstitutional or unenforceable insofar as they interfere with the creation of a system providing for equal education within a geographic metropolitan area, and for the court to enjoin defendants from depriving complainants of an equal education."

Named as defendants were the Edgewood Independent School District and all the districts surrounding Edgewood, including Harlandale, Northside, North East, Alamo Heights, San Antonio, and South San Antonio. Also named in Gochman's complaint was Crawford C. Martin, attorney general for the State of Texas. Martin was included because, as the state's chief law-enforcement official, he was responsible for administering the laws allegedly denying an equal education to the Edgewood children. There was, however, an additional benefit to having Crawford Martin as a defendant: naming a state official might allow Gochman to argue that this case ought to be heard by a three-judge district court.

Usually, a single judge presides over a federal district court. Around the turn of the twentieth century, however, Congress began passing statutes mandating three-judge courts — consisting of two federal district court judges and one judge from the court of appeals overseeing that particular district — in certain situations. Prior to 1976 (when the law was changed), Section 2281 of the 1948 Judicial Code called for a three-judge district court to be impaneled whenever a state official was enjoined from enforcing a state law on the grounds that the law violated the federal Constitution.

Section 2281 was grounded in what Justice Hugo Black called "our federalism." As a matter of law and history, the federal government is supposed to respect state sovereignty. When a district court, as an agent of the federal government, overrides a state law, this represents an exception to the deference normally given to states. Of course, under the Supremacy Clause of Article VI of the Constitution (declaring the Constitution and federal laws and treaties passed under the Constitution's authority to be supreme over state constitutions and laws), this deference is not absolute. Nevertheless, given the seriousness of the federalism questions raised by overturning a state law on federal grounds, Congress thought that the initial responsibility for making such a determination was too great to be given to a single judge. As explained by the late Charles Alan Wright, who was the nation's reigning expert on federal procedure (and who, ironically, was enlisted by the State of Texas to argue *Rodriguez* before the Supreme Court), "it was the thought of Congress that there would be less public resentment if enforcement of the state statute were stayed by three judges rather than one, and that the provision for direct appeal to the Supreme Court would provide speedy review."

As Wright had noticed, one of the advantages of obtaining review by a three-judge district court was that adverse decisions could be appealed directly to the Supreme Court. Not only would the court of appeals be bypassed (one court of appeals judge already having sat on the initial panel), but the Supreme Court would have very little discretion when determining whether to hear the appeal.

Arthur Gochman, however, saw an additional benefit in bringing this particular case to a three-judge court. In the years following *Brown v. Board of Education* (1954), the Court of Appeals for the Fifth Circuit had championed desegregation efforts. Since *Rodriguez* involved both race and education, and was thus arguably connected to *Brown*, Gochman had suspected that a judge from that court might be sympathetic to his argument. Of course, the only way to make sure that one of the Fifth Circuit judges heard his evidence in full would be to have a three-judge district court assigned to hear his complaint.

Regardless of whether *Rodriguez* would ultimately be decided by a three-judge court, initially the case would have to be assigned to a single judge. Gochman was fortunate; his case was given to Judge Adrian Anthony Spears, chief judge for the Western District of Texas. The fifty-eight-year-old jurist had been on the bench since 1961, nominated by President Kennedy to fill a newly created vacancy on the district court. Since then he had developed a reputation for fairness and professionalism. Gochman was confident that, if he could make a case, he might be able to grab Spears's vote.

As was normal in such situations, the defendants in *Rodriguez* immediately sought to have the case dismissed "for failure to state a claim upon which relief may be granted." When the first hearing on this matter was held on November 14, Gochman was prepared with an answer. He immediately brought up *Hobson v. Hansen* (1967). Had not Judge Skelly Wright granted relief in that case? Gochman suggested that the situation in Edgewood was identical to what had happened in Washington, D.C. For this was not just a case of unequal funding; in San Antonio, as in Washington, D.C., race was a factor. Gochman explained to the court "that under the Fourteenth Amendment the courts will tolerate differences relating to people that are in the same category, historically, but that the courts will not tolerate differences where there has been historical discrimination as stated in *Hobson v. Hansen*, that the courts will look closely at discrimination if it involves the poor or minority groups." It would have been a different situation, argued Gochman, if Bexar (pronounced "beyar") county, which included all the named school districts "was all white, Anglo-Saxon, [and] Protestant."

This emphasis on the nexus of wealth and race in Judge Wright's decision in *Hobson* would prove valuable to Gochman. The day after the hearing, a case was handed down by a three-judge district court in Illinois that, on its face, was very similar to *Rodriguez. McInnis v. Shapiro* (1968) had been brought by students from Cook County, Illinois, against Samuel Shapiro, then governor of that state, and other state officials. The students claimed that the education funding laws in Illinois violated the Fourteenth Amendment "because they [permitted] wide variations in the expenditures per student from district to district, thereby providing some students with a good education and depriving others, who have equal or greater educational need." On November 15, 1968, a three-judge district court ruled unanimously against the students. The court explained that the Supreme Court had never inter-

{ *Chapter 4* }

preted the Equal Protection Clause to prohibit states from passing laws that resulted in some inequality of treatment. Moreover, the court felt that it was almost impossible to define "educational need" in such a way that it was amenable to traditional analysis under the Fourteenth Amendment. Finally, even if it was determined that a violation of that amendment had occurred, the court questioned whether there existed any "judicially manageable standards" that might serve as a remedy.

On March 24, 1969, the Supreme Court, without offering an opinion, summarily upheld the judgment of the Illinois federal court. Lawyers for the North East Independent School District in San Antonio quickly filed a motion bringing this decision to the attention of Judge Spears. If Gochman expected to win in district court, he would have to be able to distinguish *Rodriguez* from *McInnis*. The fact that, unlike *Hobson*, *McInnis* did not involve a racial element might be crucial.

Before even addressing the challenge posed by *McInnis*, however, Judge Spears had to make a decision about whether to request that a three-judge court be impaneled. Initially, he was reluctant to act, being unsure of whether Attorney General Martin should in fact be named as a party to the case, since he had no direct role in school funding. Then, on January 10, 1969, Judge Spears agreed to contact Judge John R. Brown, then chief judge for the Fifth Circuit, to request that a three-judge panel be named. Spears changed his mind because of a decision Judge Brown had rendered a few months earlier in *Jackson v. Choate* (1968). In that case, Brown had written "whether the question presented is properly a three-judge matter is initially for the determination of a three-judge court." In response to Spears's request, Judge Brown about a week later designated his colleague on the Fifth Circuit, Judge Irving L. Goldberg, along with district court Judge Jack Roberts, to join Spears on a three-judge panel. Still, the impaneling of a three-judge court was not a final determination on the issue. In fact, on May 12, Judge Spears, speaking now on behalf of the entire three-judge court, concluded that "in the present posture of this case, this is a one-judge, not a three-judge matter." Since the case was still developing, however, Spears concluded that it was wise to have the three-judge panel continue to hear oral arguments, just in case the "present posture" of the case should change.

So, on June 16, all three judges convened to hear arguments and to consider implications of the Supreme Court's affirming of *McInnis*. In his initial questions to Gochman, Judge Spears directed attention to the court's opinion of May 12, in which the court had rejected the call for a three-judge panel, arguing that in all the three-judge cases involving schools heretofore decided, board of education members, not just the state's attorney general, had been included as defendants. Spears referred to these as "left-handed suggestions that, maybe, perhaps these other people might be proper parties" and asked "why haven't you done anything about that?" Gochman responded, meekly, that he did not think that the court would allow him to add new parties to the case. In a reply that probably shocked Gochman, Spears suggested: "You can't ever assume that you are not going to get anything unless you ask for it." Gochman now knew how to get his case before all three judges: All he had to do was to name the Texas Board of Education as a defendant.

The next issue addressed at the hearing was the impact the *McInnis* case ought to have on *Rodriguez*. Gochman had studied the Illinois case and believed that he had identified a crucial difference. He explained to the court that, in *McInnis*, the districts involved had different costs. Therefore, it was difficult for the court in that case to determine whether the differences in funding led to actual inequalities. Perhaps less money was needed in lower-cost districts. All the school districts that had been named by Gochman in his complaint, however, were in approximately the same place. Insofar as they all had the same costs, differences in funding would necessarily result in unequal performance. Then Gochman moved back to *Hobson*, reminding the court that "there is discrimination. . . . against the poor and against the racial minority, and the boundary line which sets this discrimination has no justification for being where it is today."

Ralph Langley represented one of the named defendants, the North East Independent School District, at the June 16 hearing. When it was his turn to speak, he focused his argument directly on *Hobson*. By this time, Abe Fortas had already been forced to resign from the Court, and Warren Burger had replaced Earl Warren as chief justice. Langley referred the district court to what he called the en banc "reformation" of Judge Skelly Wright's opinion in *Hobson*. What was most interesting, said Langley, was the new chief justice's dissent (issued while Burger still sat on the Court of Appeals for the District of Columbia Circuit). Langley asked the court "to consider with me Mr. Chief Justice Burger's language." He read aloud the quote that the new chief justice had pulled from the *Harvard Law Review*, which criticized virtually every aspect of Skelly Wright's opinion in *Hobson*. The implication should have been clear to everyone in the courtroom, especially Arthur Gochman: No matter what happened at the district court level, when the case got to the Supreme Court, the Edgewood parents should not expect a warm reception from at least one important member of that body.

Throughout the summer of 1969, motions continued to fly back and forth between the parties. Heeding Judge Spears's advice, Gochman amended his complaint to include the Texas commissioner of education, the members of the Texas Board of Education, and the Bexar County school trustees. The individual school districts responded with motions to be dismissed from the case. The districts felt that this had now become a case with statewide ramifications, and it was unfair to expect any of the individual school districts to bear the legal expenses. On October 15, Spears finally issued an order in the case. He accepted the additional defendants and dismissed the individual school districts. Since proper defendants had now been named, the May 12 decision rejecting the use of a three-judge panel was reversed. Finally, the judge overruled the motion to dismiss the case.

## Two-Year Delay

As Gochman read through the order, it must have seemed to him that he had won the first round. He would be able to argue the merits of his case, and on the bench as part of the three-judge panel would be Judge Irving Goldberg from the Fifth Circuit Court of Appeals. But, at the end of the order, Judge Spears had made a crucial determination. House Bill 240, passed by the Texas legislature during its prior session, had authorized the formation of a committee charged with recommending "a specific formula or formulae to establish a fair and equitable basis for the division of the financial responsibility between the state and the various local school districts of Texas." This committee was named the "Legislative Interim Committee on State-Local Relationships in Financing the Minimum Foundation School Program" and was eventually chaired by Senator A. M. Aiken, Jr., who had been responsible for the earlier Gilmer-Aiken legislation, and who was considered an expert on school finance issues. Spears felt that the state legislature, and not a federal district court, was the proper body to change the state's school financing system. He therefore decided, upon learning about the state committee, to stay the proceedings until after the next legislative session. The Texas legislature, however, only met once every two years, and was not scheduled to convene for another fifteen months.

The period between October of 1969, when the district court issued its stay, and December of 1971, when the three-judge panel finally heard oral arguments in *Rodriguez*, was eventful. At first, things seemed to be moving in a negative direction for Gochman. On February 24, 1970, the U.S. Supreme Court affirmed a decision by a three-judge district court in Virginia, rejecting an equal protection challenge to that state's school funding formula. The case, *Burruss v. Wilkerson* (1969), had been brought by parents and students from Bath County, Virginia, against members of the Virginia Board of Education. The *Burruss* court relied entirely on *McInnis*, reasoning that although the plaintiffs' goals were "commendable beyond measure," the facts of *McInnis* "[were] scarcely distinguishable from the facts here."

The Texas legislature, perhaps believing that the three-judge court in San Antonio would rule in its favor based on *McInnis* and *Burruss*, failed to act. Bills were proposed that would have led to the elimination of the local funding portion of the Minimum Foundation Program and revised the economic index. They were not placed on the front burner, however, and when the Texas legislature adjourned in June of 1971, no progress had been made.

Then, in July of that same year, another decision was handed down that was potentially much more devastating to the *Rodriguez* plaintiffs. Although MALDEF had refused Arthur Gochman's plea to take over *Rodriguez*, in 1969 the group brought a separate case to district court on behalf of a different group of Edgewood parents and students. The case, *Guerra v. Smith* (1969), involved a very similar complaint, alleging that the Texas school financing system violated the Equal Protection Clause. The only difference between it and *Rodriguez* was that *Guerra* was heard by a single judge. On July 20, that judge issued a brief one-page order dismissing the case based on the Supreme Court affirmation of *McInnis*. The judge who issued the opinion was Jack Roberts — who was also on the three-judge panel in *Rodriguez*.

Then, on August 30, just when the situation looked hopeless, *Serrano v. Priest* was handed down by the California Supreme Court. To understand why *Serrano* was so important to *Rodriguez*, it is necessary to recall how the two-tier test had been applied. Generally, a plaintiff hoping to win an equal protection case needed a court to apply the strict scrutiny standard. Under this legal test, the "burden of proof" was clearly upon the state, which had to demonstrate that whatever action taken was necessary to advancing a compelling state interest. Only rarely is a state able to overcome the application of this standard.

The decision of whether to apply strict scrutiny is guided by precedents, or prior cases that had been decided by courts, especially the U.S. Supreme Court. By the late 1960s, Supreme Court precedents indicated that strict scrutiny would only be applied when a fundamental right had been violated or a suspect or "invidious" classification had been made by the state. Consequently, there were two approaches available to plaintiffs in school funding cases. First, they could argue that education was a fundamental right. Some support for this line of attack could be found in Chief Justice Warren's majority opinion in *Brown*. Still, *Brown* had not explicitly acknowledged a fundamental right to education. Therefore, an alternative line of attack might have been necessary. If it could have been determined that school funding schemes discriminated against a suspect class, then strict scrutiny would be applied even without a finding that education was within the narrow category of rights given fundamental status. On their face, however, school funding schemes were neutral formulas. They did not target individuals for disparate treatment. Nevertheless, if the school funds available were tied to local wealth, then those bringing a challenge could allege that, by relying on local monies, the state had "guaranteed" that those who resided in poor districts would have schools that received less money per student. On this basis, it could have been argued that the state had created a wealth-based classification.

There were two potential pitfalls to this approach. First, in school funding cases, it is difficult to identify a specific group of people who are the subjects of discriminatory action based on their lack of wealth. It is always possible that people who might be identified as "poor" live in a school district rich in property wealth. Alternatively, wealthy individuals might reside in "property poor" districts. Hence one has to argue either that a geographic unit is the victim of discrimination based on "its" relative wealth — a rather odd claim — or that individuals, regardless of personal income, can still be subject to wealth discrimination.

Even if this problem could be overcome, there remained the question of whether classifications based on wealth were "suspect" in the constitutional sense; that is, that they were among the type of distinctions triggering strict scrutiny. This was not at all clear during the period when *Rodriguez* was proceeding through the courts. In fact, part of the significance of *Rodriguez* lies in that the case provides an answer to what was then an open question regarding wealth-based classifications. Gochman's emphasis on *Hobson*, with its link between wealth and race, implied an acceptance of the argument that only racial distinctions led to the invocation of strict scrutiny.

With the California Supreme Court's 6–1 decision in *Serrano v. Priest*, there was now a case that could be cited in which many of these hurdles had been overcome. The California justices had concluded that U.S. Supreme Court precedents mandated strict scrutiny in cases involving wealth-based discrimination. The state supreme court got around the problem of defining a class for equal protection purposes by accepting that there was "a correlation between a district's per pupil assessed valuation and the wealth of its residents." Therefore, the justices were able to conclude that discrimination against a poor district was necessarily discrimination against poor individuals. Next, the California court asserted that education, if not a fundamental right, was recognized as a fundamental interest based on its close connection to another such interest — voting — which had already been recognized by the U.S. Supreme Court.

In rendering its decision that the California school finance system violated the Equal Protection Clause of the Fourteenth Amendment, the *Serrano* majority had basically accepted the road map laid out by Coons, Clune, and Sugarman. This allowed the court to reject the conclusions of both *McInnis* and *Burruss* that judicially manageable standards were unavailable in school funding cases.

The success of the Coons team's approach in *Serrano* came as a surprise to Arthur Gochman. He had focused on *Hobson*, and was barely aware of *Serrano* as it moved through the California system. In fact, the day after the *Serrano* decision was released, Gochman called Judge Spears's office asking for the judge's permission to speak to the press. Spears was not in, and Gochman left a message requesting the judge's opinion, and explaining that he did not know "anything more about the *Serrano* case than what has been in the newspaper." He would, however, prove to be a quick study, for it was becoming clear that *Serrano* would be a very useful precedent. By October of 1971, the federal district court for the District of Minnesota had released an opinion (*Van Dusartz v. Hatfield* [1971]) that strongly reinforced *Serrano*. As Judge Lord, who wrote the decision in the Minnesota case, explained it:

> The issue posed by the children, here as in *Serrano*, is whether pupils in publicly financed elementary and secondary schools enjoy a right under the equal protection guarantee of the Fourteenth Amendment to have the level of spending for their education unaffected by variations in the taxable wealth of their school district or their parents. This court concludes that such a right indeed exists. . . . Plainly put, the rule is that the level of spending for a child's education may not be a function of wealth other than the wealth of the state.

The decision cited the recently published book by Coons, Sugarman, and Clune, *Private Wealth and Public Education*. Importantly, the Minnesota court pointed out that *McInnis* and *Burruss* could be differentiated because in those cases, the state had been asked to respond to "educational need." *Van Dusartz*, like *Serrano*, was about the "right to mere fiscal neutrality."

Two days after *Serrano* was handed down, there was another twist in the *Rodriguez* case. A few weeks earlier, Judge William Wayne Justice, a federal district court judge in Tyler, Texas, had issued a ruling ordering the merging of the Del Rio and San Felipe Independent School Districts. The consolidation was mandated in order to further desegregation efforts in Texas. San Felipe was a mostly Mexican American school district. Like Edgewood, it contained an Air Force base. For many years, dependents of those who worked at the base had been bussed into the more affluent Del Rio school district. The original case in Tyler arose because San Felipe objected to the revenue loss that resulted from the transfers. Following Judge Justice's consolidation order, seven residents from Edgewood — which also had a history of bussing Air Force base dependents into wealthier districts — petitioned the district court in

Tyler asking to join the original suit, requesting an order consolidating the Edgewood and San Antonio Independent School Districts.

The developments in Tyler worried Judge Spears. As he saw it, the same issues were involved in each case, and he did not think that it would be helpful if two federal courts issued potentially conflicting judgments. Since *Rodriguez* had already been before him for several years, Spears thought it ought to take precedence. He immediately summoned the parties to the Tyler case into his courtroom for a special hearing. After the hearing, Spears asked Judge Justice to reject the motion of the Edgewood residents. Eventually, Justice conceded to Spears's request.

With the exception of the development in Tyler, things seemed to be moving in the right direction for Arthur Gochman. With the decisions in *Serrano* and *Van Dusartz*, he now had two strong precedents that he could add to *Hobson*. Since the Texas legislature had failed to take advantage of Spears's stay to pass school funding reform, it was time to get ready for the trial.

---

## Gathering the Evidence

It was now the fall of 1971 and two years had passed since Judge Spears had issued his stay. By the time *Rodriguez* was heard by the Supreme Court, this would prove to be a significant obstacle for Arthur Gochman, for he would be facing a very different Court than was in place when he had first filed the case in 1968. Before he could think about the Supreme Court, however, Gochman first had to make his case before the three-judge district court in Texas. He decided to rely on the testimony of six witnesses. This was not the type of case in which witnesses actually took the stand. Instead, written affidavits were taken and the witnesses were then deposed by opposing counsel.

The *Hobson* and *Serrano* precedents were not entirely consistent with each other. Judge Skelly Wright had assumed that unequal funding, absent any corresponding racial connection, was insufficient in itself to render a school finance plan unconstitutional. In *Serrano*, however, race had not been a factor. Gochman apparently felt that he did not have to choose between cases. He would argue both race and wealth, and demonstrate through the affidavits that school districts with low property values were unable to raise as much money for their schools as rich districts. Then, he would present evidence of a correlation between the money available for schools in San Antonio area districts and the racial composition of the districts. Finally, he would draw attention to the fact that the lack of money in the poorer districts had real consequences when it came to the equality of facilities and staff.

Jose Cardenas, superintendent of the Edgewood schools, provided the first affidavit. Cardenas provided data Gochman could use to demonstrate how a lack of funding translated into inferior schools. Cardenas used the North East Independent School District as his comparison. The wealthier district was able to provide larger classrooms, more library books, and a more consistent staff of teachers (Edgewood was forced to replace one-third of its teachers every school year because of lower pay scales). The result, claimed Cardenas, was that almost 32 percent of Edgewood students dropped out between grades seven and twelve. In the North East district, only 8 percent of the students left before being graduated from high school.

Next to testify were two economics professors, Don Webb from Trinity University in San Antonio, Texas, and Daniel Morgan from the University of Texas at Austin. Webb's testimony was important in the context of *Serrano*. He argued that those in poor districts were making a strong effort, as evidenced by the high tax rates they set for themselves, to provide a quality education for their children. Morgan then explained that this was so because "poor districts are systematically incapable of raising as many education dollars as rich districts — despite higher tax efforts in the former districts." Morgan also pointed out that the Minimum Foundation Program benefited rich districts because they were able to hire more highly qualified teachers. The state aid schedule for teachers in Texas was tied to teacher qualifications, with more money provided per teacher for better qualified teachers.

Since the early twentieth century, social science data had played an increasingly important role in the law and, by mid-century, in education cases. Chief Justice Warren's opinion in *Brown*, for example, had cited psychologist Kenneth Clarke's research in which he was able to demonstrate the effect that segregation had on the perceptions of black children. In *Hobson*, the plaintiffs' argument had been greatly enhanced by their ability to present tables illustrating the correlation between race and student spending in the District of Columbia. All of this had not been lost on Gochman. That was why he enlisted the services of Webb and Morgan. But what Gochman really needed was data that demonstrated very specifically the relationship between race, district wealth, and school performance in Texas. In a sense, he needed his own version of Kenneth Clarke. He found that person at Syracuse University. His name was Joel Berke.

Berke was an adjunct professor of political science at Syracuse University in New York. More significantly, however, he served as the director of the Educational Finance and Governance Program of the Policy Institute for the Syracuse University Research Corporation. Two years before, Berke had received a grant from the Ford Foundation to study school funding at both the national and state level. As part of his research, Berke had looked specifically at six states, including Texas. Berke and his team had sampled data from 110 Texas school districts. At Gochman's request, Berke organized the collected data into tables that allowed the court to visualize the funding situation in Texas. These tables were then made part of Berke's affidavit.

In his first table, Berke paired the percentage of Mexican Americans in a school district with the amount of money available per student in that same district. The results are shown in Table 4.1.

Recalling Judge Skelly Wright's decision in *Hobson*, one can see why Berke's data was important: it established a link between race and

Table 4.1  Expenditures per pupil

| Percent Mexican American of District Enrollment | Districts in Sample | | Estimates for All Districts | |
|---|---|---|---|---|
| | Number of Districts | Per Pupil Expenditures | Number of Districts | Per Student State and Local Expenditures |
| 10–19.9 | 55 | $457 | 85 | $444 |
| 20–29.9 | 38 | $484 | 59 | $477 |
| 30–49.9 | 32 | $444 | 49 | $444 |
| 50–79.9 | 39 | $377 | 60 | $382 |
| 80–100 | 23 | $292 | 30 | $297 |

school spending. Districts that had a Mexican American student population under 20 percent had about one-third more money to spend per student than districts in which the Mexican American student population was more than 80 percent. The problem with the data, however, is evident after even a casual glance at the chart. A significant drop-off in funding does not occur until the Mexican American student population crosses 50 percent. This caused an anomaly in the data in which funding per student actually increased slightly as the proportion of Mexican American students moved beyond 20 percent.

But Berke had more data. He was able, for example, to demonstrate empirically the problem that Morgan had presented by showing the wide gap in the amount of money that a "property poor" district could raise when compared with a district that had more property wealth. Table 4.2 shows this remains true even when a poor district taxes itself at twice the rate of a rich district.

Anticipating the state's argument that these inequities were ameliorated by state and federal funding dollars, Berke illustrated in Table 4.3 how this inability to generate revenue led to large differences in per student spending, even after these other funds were factored into the data.

Table 4.2  District wealth, tax effort, and tax yield

| Market Value of Taxable Property Per Student | Equalized Tax Rates on $100 | Yield Per Student (Equalized Rate Applied to District Market Value) |
|---|---|---|
| Above $100,000 (10 Districts) | $0.31 | $585 |
| $100,000–$50,000 (26 Districts) | $0.38 | $262 |
| $50,000–$30,000 (30 Districts) | $0.55 | $213 |
| $30,000–$10,000 (40 Districts) | $0.72 | $162 |
| Below $10,000 (4 Districts) | $0.70 | $60 |

Table 4.3 District wealth and school revenue

| Market Value Taxable Property Per Student | Local Revenues Per Student | State Revenues Per Student | State and Local Revenues Per Student (Columns 1 And 2) | Federal Revenues Per Student | Total Revenues Per Student (State-Local-Federal, Columns 1, 2, and 4) |
|---|---|---|---|---|---|
| Above $100,000 (10 Districts) | $610 | $205 | $815 | $41 | $856 |
| $100,000–$50,000 (26 Districts) | $287 | $257 | $544 | $66 | $610 |
| $50,000–$30,000 (30 Districts) | $224 | $260 | $484 | $45 | $529 |
| $30,000–$10,000 (40 Districts) | $166 | $295 | $461 | $85 | $546 |
| Below $10,000 (4 Districts) | $63 | $243 | $305 | $135 | $441 |

Finally, Berke provided a table that integrated his earlier findings with the presentations of both Cardenas and Morgan (Table 4.4). The inability of districts like Edgewood that lacked property wealth to raise money, regardless of tax rates, led to worse educational quality. For example, in Edgewood, the district with the least amount of money to spend per student, only 15 percent of the teachers had obtained a master's degree and almost half were not fully certified, instead teaching with emergency permits. In Alamo Heights, the richest district in the San Antonio area, more than twice as many teachers had master's degrees and almost 90 percent were fully certified.

Here is how Joel Berke summarized his data:

> [W]e conclude that the system of school finance in Texas makes the quality of education a direct function of the wealth of local school districts, providing consistently higher quality schooling in districts with higher property values per pupil and consistently lower quality education in school systems with less local resources available for taxation. Furthermore, our study demonstrates that poorer districts tax themselves at consistently higher equalized tax rates yet realize far lower tax yields than is true in the richer districts. . . . Racial discrimination is also readily apparent. . . . There is a consistent pattern of higher quality education in districts with higher proportions of Anglo-Americans.

Pat Bailey, assistant attorney general in Texas, was assigned to represent the state in this case. It was, therefore, his job to depose Gochman's experts. In his questioning, Bailey demonstrated that *Rodriguez* was about more than just wealth, race, and education. Although he tried to discredit some of Berke's results, his focus was on the political aspects of the case.

When discussing the politics inherent in school funding cases, it is common to think that the only issues are tax-related. Wealthy voters are understandably reluctant to pay high taxes, particularly if the resulting revenue is to be spent purchasing goods that appear not to directly benefit them. To the degree that they can influence legislators, they will try to get the state government to avoid equalization measures. Therefore, school funding debates are just another example of disputes that typically arise in the realm of domestic politics. During the Cold War, however, such debates could be transformed into

Table 4.4 District wealth and educational quality

| Selected Districts from High to Low by Market Valuation Per Student | Professional Salaries Per Student | Percent Teachers with | | Percent of Total Staff with Emergency Permits | Student Counselor Ratios | Professional Personnel Per 100 Students |
| --- | --- | --- | --- | --- | --- | --- |
| | | College Degrees | Masters Degrees | | | |
| ALAMO HEIGHTS | $372.00 | 100 | 40 | 11 | 645 | 4.80 |
| NORTH EAST | $288.00 | 99 | 24 | 7 | 1516 | 4.50 |
| SAN ANTONIO | $251.00 | 98 | 29 | 17 | 2320 | 4.0 |
| NORTHSIDE | $258.00 | 99 | 20 | 17 | 1493 | 4.30 |
| HARLANDALE | $243.00 | 94 | 21 | 22 | 1800 | 4.00 |
| EDGEWOOD | $209.00 | 96 | 15 | 47 | 3098 | 4.06 |

something more. Any political program that called for the transfer of wealth from one group to another under the auspices of equalization resembled some policies that could be associated with Soviet communism or socialism (the terms were often used interchangeably). Rhetorically, the charge of communism or socialism was an effective political trump card. And this was a card that the State of Texas was more than willing to play.

To realize this, one only need read the transcripts of the depositions conducted by Bailey. For example, here is a portion of the deposition of Daniel Morgan:

Bailey: "Doctor Morgan, you say that you don't want one district to be able to afford a much greater educational opportunity than what may be afforded by some other districts. How are you ever going to do this unless you put some ceilings on it, Doctor Morgan?"

Morgan: "Well, one of the approaches you can take is what — it has many, many terms, political economy approach, Wisconsin approach — by making the same kind of effort they can come to the same revenue. In other words, equalize fiscal power, fiscal potential, power equalizing, whatever you want to say."

Bailey: "Socialism?"

Morgan: (laughing) "Yes. Public schools are — if you want to say public schools are social, public social principle, I will be happy to say that. I will call it capitalism, if you want to. If you want to say socialism, I will say public school education is socialism."

Bailey took the same approach with Jose Cardenas.

Bailey: "In other words, you don't think we ought to do this unless they raise everybody's standards as much?"

Cardenas: "That's right."

Bailey: "In other words, everybody shares equally?"

Cardenas: "Yes."

Bailey: "I reckon that has a name to it."

The state's focus on the socialist underpinnings of any attempt to equalize school funding eventually led to a rather comic moment.

Richard Avena, then director of the Southwestern Field Office for the U.S. Commission on Civil Rights, had offered an affidavit establishing that school district lines had been drawn with an eye to race. During his deposition, Bailey asked suspiciously why as a young man Avena had spent some time in South America. Bailey, who apparently was expecting to hear tales of Avena cavorting with Che Guevara, was disappointed to learn that, instead, the young man had been a Mormon missionary.

## The Case Is Finally Heard

With the California court's decision in *Serrano*, the wealthier school districts in San Antonio took a renewed interest in *Rodriguez*. The North East Independent School District, which had brought *McInnis* to the attention of Judge Spears, and which had subsequently asked to be dismissed from the case, now asked to be allowed to intervene. The motion was denied, but the North East, Harlandale, Alamo Heights, and Northside Independent School Districts were eventually allowed to participate as *amicus curiae* (friends of the court).

Gochman had by this time enlisted the help of two other attorneys: Rose Spector, who, like Gochman, was an attorney in San Antonio (she would go on to serve on the Texas Supreme Court), and University of Texas law professor Mark Yudof.

In the fall of 1969, Yudof had gone to the Harvard Center for Law and Education to work with several lawyers and professors concerned with developing a litigation strategy (similar to what the NAACP had done in the area of school segregation) for school finance cases. Yudof assisted in organizing the arguments and helped write briefs. He participated in the New Jersey school finance case, *Robinson v. Cahill* (1973) and worked on an amicus curie brief filed in *Serrano*. When he learned about the case in San Antonio, he contacted Gochman, told him that he taught a course at University of Texas Law School in educational law, and offered to work on the brief with him. Gochman did not know at that time that Yudof had been involved in the *Serrano* litigation. Nevertheless, he welcomed his help.

Yudof's involvement in *Rodriguez* was important. There was some consternation on the part of those who had been involved in these school funding cases throughout the country, and who had an organized strategy, that Gochman, who was not an academic and who did not travel in their circles, had jumped ahead of the pack. Unlike Gochman, Yudof knew and had worked with Coons, Sugarman, and Clune. He would therefore serve as a somewhat behind-the-scenes link to *Serrano*.

Yudof's influence can be seen in Gochman's slow turn away from race and toward wealth as the defining state classification involved in the Texas school financing system. Yudof was convinced that, especially in Texas, an emphasis on race would fail, since it could too easily be countered by arguments that poverty and race were not necessarily linked. Even Berke's data failed to establish a definitive link.

Still, Gochman was not willing to give up on *Hobson* as a precedent. Indeed, Gochman's determination to fuse *Hobson* and *Serrano* was evident in his trial brief submitted to the court in early November. In defining the class represented by the plaintiffs, the brief specifically noted that it included those "who are American of Mexican descent." Also represented were "all other persons in Texas who have school children in independent school districts who are members of minority groups or are poor." This took care of *Hobson*. Then, showing Yudof's influence, the brief moved to *Serrano*, explaining that the problem with the Texas school financing system was that "the quality of a child's education [was] a function of the wealth of his parents and neighbors, as measured by the tax base of the school district in which said child resides."

Near the end of the brief, Gochman suggested potential remedies that the court might order. Citing both *Serrano* and *Van Dusartz*, the brief argued that the "clear, effective, and moderate" standard by which the court should be guided was that "the quality of public education may not be a function of wealth other than the wealth of the state as a whole." This was right out of the Coons, Sugarman, and Clune book. On his copy of the brief, Judge Spears wrote in the margin next to the phrase "clear, effective, and moderate," the words "not true."

The hearing before Judges Spears, Goldberg, and Roberts took place on the morning of December 10, 1971. Gochman spoke first. His argument began on a light-hearted note when Spears, who had been asked by Judge Goldberg (from the Fifth Circuit) to run the case, asked him whether Rose Spector would be participating in the argument. Before Spears could even complete the question Gochman answered that he would "do all the arguing," and that "she will tell me what I did wrong afterwards."

The tone of the hearing immediately turned more serious, however, as Gochman brought up the most damaging precedent for his side of the case, *McInnis*. He tried to convince the judges that since *McInnis* had already been affirmed by the Supreme Court when the district court rejected the earlier motion to dismiss, this implied agreement with the brief he had submitted at that time. That brief had sought to distinguish *McInnis* from *Rodriguez*. Spears immediately rejected this line of reasoning and instructed Gochman that he had best address both *McInnis* and *Burruss* since "we are a three-judge court in the federal system and the Supreme Court did affirm both *McInnis* and *Burrus*." In response, Gochman pointed out that the plaintiffs in *McInnis* had asked that educational spending be tied to student needs. This was what had led the three-judge court in the Illinois case to conclude that there was no judicially manageable standard available. Gochman explained that his approach did not ask the court to determine whether any student's educational needs were being met. To illustrate this, he read the quote from *Private Wealth and Public Education* used in his brief, which stated only that "the quality of education cannot be a function of wealth except for the wealth of the state as a whole." The precedent for this standard was of course *Serrano*, but as Gochman mentioned the California case, Judge Goldberg cut him off, pointing out that, unlike *McInnis*, *Serrano* had not been affirmed by the U.S. Supreme Court. Indeed, no appeal had been taken by California, so there would be no possibility of *Serrano* being affirmed by the Supreme Court.

Goldberg then questioned whether Gochman was giving a fair reading to the Illinois case since, although *McInnis* was about educational needs, it was also about expenditures. The difference, countered Gochman, was that under an educational needs standard, courts would be forced to strictly examine what was occurring in each school district. The reason this was such a "moderate" standard — the term to which Spears objected in Gochman's brief — is that it only looked at funding schemes. As long as poor districts were able to raise as much money as rich districts, the courts would be satisfied. Gochman offered as evidence for the current problem the fact that Alamo Heights was able to spend almost twice as much money per student than Edgewood, even though Edgewood had a higher tax rate.

Temporarily accepting Gochman's point, Judge Goldberg then raised the next logical question. Even if *Rodriguez* advocated a "moderate" standard of wealth equalization, why should any equalization at all be demanded under the Fourteenth Amendment? The implication of the judge's question was that wealth-based classifications were not to be strictly scrutinized under the Equal Protection Clause. Gochman was ready with a reply. He cited the first footnote in the Fifth Circuit case of *Hawkins v. Town of Shaw* (1971). In that case, the court of appeals had overturned a lower court ruling, finding that the town of Shaw, Mississippi, had discriminated based on race when providing various municipal services. Although the case turned on racial discrimination, Judge Tuttle, who wrote for the appellate panel, claimed in the footnote Gochman referenced "that the Supreme Court has stated that wealth as well as race renders a classification highly suspect and thus demanding of more exacting judicial scrutiny." The footnote was based on Chief Justice Warren's opinion in *McDonald v. Board of Election Commissioners of Chicago* (1969), but Gochman had good reason to cite the Fifth Circuit case instead: Judge Goldberg had been a member of the appellate panel that decided *Shaw* and the decision had been unanimous.

Rather than being convinced by the reference to a case in which he had participated, Judge Goldberg dismissed the case as a precedent, pointing out that *Shaw* was about race, and asking Gochman: "Are you predicating your whole case here on the theory that there is ethnicity involved?" Gochman acknowledged that ethnicity was involved, but admitted that his case was "based on wealth," and that he wanted the court to "give scrutiny to classifications based on wealth."

After sparring with Goldberg over whether the Supreme Court precedents distinguished education from other government entitlements, Gochman once again faced questions from Spears. The judge wanted to get to the core of Gochman's argument and asked which legal test he thought the court should apply. In his question, Spears referred to strict scrutiny as the "compelling state interest test." In his answer, Gochman covered all of his bases by saying that "the compelling state interest test applies, but we say there is not rational basis even for the present Texas system because local people cannot do what they want to do under the present system." The implication was that even if the lower tier of scrutiny was applied, the State of Texas would lose.

After explaining to the court that in the prior legislative session "nothing happened" in the area of school finance, Gochman sat down. Pat Bailey, assistant attorney general, then argued on behalf of his boss, Texas Attorney General Crawford Martin. Judge Spears followed up on Gochman's last point by asking Bailey to tell the court whether the legislature had done anything in the time granted them by the district court. Bailey tried to talk around the obvious lack of progress, arguing that a committee was still working on the problem. This clearly did not satisfy the judge, who replied that it seemed as if the legislature would take no action "unless they are forced to do it." Bailey suggested that the court needed to be more patient and criticized those who "cry out that for every problem the Constitution requires an answer." Even if there was a problem with how schools were financed in Texas, Bailey argued, the conclusion of *McInnis* was that this was not the type of situation that courts should or could resolve. When Goldberg pointed out to him that courts had gotten involved in the past with similarly complex issues — perhaps referring to the desegregation cases heard by his Fifth Circuit Court of Appeals — Bailey shifted ground and began to attack the remedy sought by the plaintiffs. He tried to convince the court that Gochman recommended not equal opportunity to raise money for schools but absolute equality in financing, whereby no school district, no matter how willing it might be to tax itself, would be allowed to spend more than another district. Judge Goldberg disagreed with this characterization of Gochman's position, but Bailey did not budge. As the assistant attorney general saw it, "they [the plaintiffs] want the same amount spent on every child; this is socialized education." Since socialism was obviously not what those who adopted the Fourteenth Amendment had in mind, Bailey argued that it was a resolution that should not be entertained by a court. Goldberg, however, continued to object to Mr. Bailey's portrayal of Gochman's proposed remedy, adding that if he was wrong, Gochman should be allowed to correct him.

Bailey, however, was not finished. He wanted to talk about the legal tests relevant to school funding. He knew that Gochman wanted strict scrutiny applied, and reminded the court that this was a test that a state could never pass. In situations such as the one at the core of this case, Bailey explained, there were no precedents available that would lead the judges to apply the higher standard. Foreshadowing much of what would become part of the Supreme Court's deliberations, he claimed that strict scrutiny originated in *Kramer v. Union School District* (1969). *Kramer* involved a situation in which a renter had been forbidden to participate in a local election. It was logical to conclude, therefore, that strict scrutiny only applied in situations such as *Kramer*, in which there was an absolute and not just a relative deprivation of a fundamental right. *Serrano*, since it had been decided by a California state court, was not, Bailey thought, binding on a federal district court in Texas. And *Van Dusartz*, the district court case from Minnesota that followed along the lines of *Serrano*, could be countered by the case brought by MALDEF, *Guerra v. Smith*. As Bailey was most likely well aware, *Guerra* had been decided by Judge Jack Roberts, who had been silent during the hearing, but who was on the panel and would be casting a vote in *Rodriguez*.

Bailey then surrendered the rest of his time to Ralph Langley, who was again representing the North East Independent School District, which had been allowed back into the case as an amicus curiae participant. Langley emphasized that, as he understood the case, Gochman was seeking complete egalitarianism in education, a standard that, if taken to its logical extreme, might eliminate private schools as well as supplemental spending on special education. As he had done to Bailey, Goldberg objected to this overstatement of the plaintiffs' position. The judge then invited Arthur Gochman to respond and state whether "if you were to prevail in this case and you were to write the decree in this case, that you would have absolute egalitarianism in the dollars per child per every student in the State of Texas." "Absolutely not," answered Gochman, who went on to explain that he was not advocating for any rigid formula. Nevertheless, Gochman did provide an example of how power equalizing might be applied in practice. "What we are saying," reiterated Gochman, "is that public school education is a state obligation and the state should devise some system where the quality of education is not totally dependent upon the wealth of the people and their neighbors."

Although *Serrano* had influenced Gochman's approach to the court, he had not abandoned *Hobson* and its concern with the intersection of wealth and race. Gochman closed by reminding the court that although the case did not turn on race, there was evidence that as the percentage of minorities rose in a district, the amount spent per student went down. Moreover, the state was partially to blame for this, having enforced home titles in wealthy neighborhoods containing clauses (known as restrictive covenants) preventing the houses from being sold to Mexican Americans.

------

## The Decision

Less than two weeks later, on Thursday, December 23, 1971, the three-judge court issued its decision in *Rodriguez*. Gochman and the Edgewood parents had won a hands-down victory. The decision was not authored by any single judge but was "per curium," meaning "for the court." Unanimously, the judges decided that the Texas school funding system violated the Equal Protection Clause of the Fourteenth Amendment. As a matter of law, the three-judge court concluded that *Serrano* and *Van Dusartz* were correctly decided and that wealth was a suspect classification triggering strict scrutiny. The court also declared, relying on *Brown v. Board of Education*, that education was a "fundamental interest," again a conclusion that led to the invocation of the higher standard. The judges went even further, however, arguing that Texas had not even demonstrated that it could meet the minimal requirements of the rational basis test.

The three-judge court was clearly unmoved by the state's assertion that what the plaintiffs requested amounted to a form of socialism. First of all, the court explained, "fiscal neutrality" (one of the terms Gochman had borrowed from Coons, Clune, and Sugarman) was different from absolute equality. The judges were not ordering that every school receive the same funding, but rather that every district be empowered to raise a similar amount regardless of local wealth. Furthermore, wrote the judges, educational funding had, as Morgan had pointed out, already "been socialized." Therefore, "[t]he *type* of socialized education, not the question of its existence, is the only matter currently in dispute."

The court ordered that the state and the other defendants be permanently enjoined from enforcing the sections of the Texas Constitution and the various Texas statutes dealing with the financing of education. This would force the state to adopt a new funding scheme since, absent any legislative response, the schools would not be allowed to continue to function in Texas. The court, however, stayed its decision for two years to give the state time to draft new laws in response to the court's order.

About a month later, on January 26, 1972, the three-judge court issued a clarification to its initial opinion in order to calm the worries of school officials and bankers who feared that, under a new financing system, districts would have to default on their prior bonded debt. The opinion now specified that the court's decision would "in no way affect the validity, incontestability, obligation to pay, source of payment or enforceability of any presently outstanding bond, note, or other security issued and delivered, or contractual obligation incurred by Texas school districts." According to Mark Yudof, who assisted Gochman in preparing the plaintiffs' case, the reaction in Texas to the three-judge court's ruling was "one of surprise bordering on shock." The opinion, although clear to those who were used to legal terminology and familiar with power equalizing, was misunderstood by the press and hence the public. There were two main concerns: First, many mistakenly thought that the three-judge court had eliminated local property taxes as a source of revenue for schools. Indeed, Judge Spears received quite a few letters from senior citizens praising the court's decision for just this reason. Others, however, feared the imposition of a statewide tax which would then be redistributed to poorer districts. Suburban schools had an additional worry. They remembered the case out of Tyler, and thought the three-judge panel was just one step away from ordering consolidation of school districts. Even before the decision was handed down, superintendents representing about forty suburban school districts gathered in Irving, Texas, and formed the Texas Association of Suburban Schools. In Alamo Heights, the wealthy school district so often used as a benchmark by the Edgewood plaintiffs, an emergency meeting was held in which a petition opposing consolidation was circulated. It was sent to the state legislature and to President Nixon.

## Appeal to the Supreme Court

Texas's political officials, however, did not react to the three-judge panel's decision. They had, after all, been given two years to respond. In the meantime, they held out hope that the Supreme Court would reverse the lower court's ruling. On April 17, 1972, the state filed its appeal with the U.S. Supreme Court.

Since *Rodriguez* had been decided by a three-judge district court, it would have been difficult for the Supreme Court to avoid reviewing the case. Indeed, this was one of the principal advantages of qualifying for a three-judge panel. Normally, a case arising in the federal system would begin in a district court, be reviewed by a court of appeals in the appropriate circuit, and then go to the Supreme Court via a petition for a writ of certiorari. In order for a writ of certiorari to be granted, at least four justices had to agree to hear the case. Writs of certiorari are granted at the discretion of the justices, and only a very small percentage of cases are actually "granted cert." and heard by the Supreme Court.

Under existing federal law at the time, cases decided by three-judge district courts came directly to the Court "on appeal." Theoretically, the Supreme Court had no discretion in such situations and had to hear the case. In such cases (which are very rare nowadays due to changes in federal law) the Court merely recognized "probable jurisdiction" and automatically reviewed the lower court's decision. This did not mean, however, that a case decided by a three-judge court always received a full hearing before the court. For example, *Burruss* and *McInnis* were both decided by three-judge courts, but were summarily affirmed, without oral argument, by the Supreme Court. Indeed, in *Van Dusartz*, the plaintiffs intentionally did not seek an injunction against state officials; instead, they asked for a mere declaration that the state was violating the Constitution, as a way of avoiding a three-judge court. Had the ruling gone against them, they might have expected an adverse summary judgment by the Supreme Court.

Gochman's strategy was different: He actively sought a three-judge panel. In part, this was because, when he started out, he was confident of a victory before the Supreme Court, and so saw no need to avoid the justices. Also, Gochman thought that he would benefit from having a judge from the Fifth Circuit participate in the initial review of his case. Perhaps if Gochman had been able to predict the changes that would take place on the nation's highest court, or the outcomes in *McInnis* and *Burruss*, he would not have been as anxious to obtain review by a three-judge district court. Nevertheless, by the time those cases were handed down, it was too late to turn back.

After Gochman's victory before the three-judge district court, there was little doubt that Texas would appeal. The only question was whether the Court would simply issue a summary judgment — perhaps a summary reversal, given its earlier decisions in *McInnis* and *Burruss* — or would allow a full hearing in the case. Because of the conflicting decisions rendered in California, Illinois, Minnesota, and Virginia, however, the Court apparently concluded that a full opinion was now necessary on this subject. At their June 5 conference, the justices decided they had jurisdiction; two days later (on the last day of the October 1971 term), the Court announced that it would hear the case.

# The Education Justice

## Justice Powell and the Importance of the Local School Board

*Rodriguez* caught the attention of at least one of the justices even before the Court formally announced it would hear the case. Justice Lewis F. Powell, Jr., at the time had only been on the Court for six months, and was still adjusting to its unfamiliar demands. Before arriving at the Court, the sixty-four-year-old justice had enjoyed a distinguished legal career working with one of the most successful and politically powerful firms in Richmond, Virginia. His focus, however, had not been on constitutional law. Although many of the issues that came to Court were new to him, *Rodriguez* was a case about education, a subject on which Powell had considerable expertise.

In the late 1940s, Powell had chaired the charter revision panel for the city of Richmond. In recognition of his work on that project, the city council appointed him to fill an unexpired term on the Richmond School Board. He was then reappointed to a full term and, in 1952, elected chair. He would hold that position until 1961, when he left to serve on the Virginia Board of Education (the same body that served as the defendant in *Burruss*). In 1968, he left the state board, having completed two four-year terms. Altogether, therefore, Powell held a leadership role in public education in Virginia for nearly twenty years.

When Powell was initially nominated to the U.S. Supreme Court by Richard Nixon, the Virginian's service on the two boards was the source of some controversy. Powell's tenure had coincided with Virginia's repeated attempts to evade the desegregation requirements of *Brown v. Board of Education* (1954). Powell's record on desegregation was at best mixed. Although he actively and effectively opposed the southern policy of "massive resistance," with its plan to close down the public schools, Powell was never a strong voice for integration. Those who opposed Powell's appointment to the court pointed out that when Powell left the Richmond School Board in 1961, only two black children (out of 23,000 African American students) attended school with whites. Powell's record on the state board was equally unimpressive, at least when it came to state efforts to desegregate the public schools.

Nevertheless, when it came time for the Senate to consider his nomination, several civil rights leaders in Virginia testified on his behalf, which mitigated the criticisms of Powell's civil rights record. Moreover, the senators were much more focused on Nixon's other nominee, William Rehnquist, so that Powell was easily confirmed. Once on the Court, Powell's years of involvement in public education served him well. For, as it turned out, *Rodriguez* would be only the first of many education decisions authored by Powell. By the time he left the Court in 1987, Powell had penned the majority opinion in more than two dozen education cases and had earned the nickname "The Education Justice."

---

## Civic Education and the Communist Threat

Powell noticed *Rodriguez* very quickly. On June 2, 1972, three days before the justices even discussed jurisdiction over the case in conference, Powell wrote a note to his clerks Larry Hammond and J. Harvie Wilkinson, III, telling them to put *Rodriguez* "on [their] summer list for study."

Powell took his own advice, and, as he would later recall, "devoted considerable time during the summer to *Rodriguez*," making "extensive notes." What he discovered worried him. Shortly before he left the Richmond School Board, Powell had given a speech to a gathering of Richmond teachers in which he reiterated his faith "in the basic soundness of the American public school system," explaining that he was "unmoved by those who urge that the European or Soviet system is better." This reference to other systems, in particular the system in place in the former Soviet Union, is telling. Powell had long before made the connection between public education and the maintenance of U.S. democracy. This view was reinforced in the summer of 1958 when Powell traveled to Moscow with other members of the American Bar Association. Upon his return, he gave a report to the Richmond School Board entitled "Soviet Education — A Means Towards World Domination." To Powell, if the Soviet educational system existed to promote communism, the American system had to be just as determined to promote freedom and democracy. Toward that end, Powell had drafted an amendment that is now part of the Virginia Constitution asserting that "free government rests . . . upon the broadest possible diffusion of knowledge." The tie to his fellow Virginian Thomas Jefferson's conception of civic education was unmistakable.

What would be accomplished if education, so intimately related to the preservation of the U.S. political system, became itself an example of socialism or communism? Assistant Attorney General Pat Bailey had raised this question when he had defended Texas against the *Rodriguez* case before the three-judge panel. If that decision was upheld, Powell suspected that it would lead to more centralized authority over education. Indeed, Powell would later share with his clerks his fear that the centralization would not stop in the state capital. If spending in Edgewood had to be equal to spending in Alamo Heights, then did Texas have to be equal to Virginia? Why stop at elementary and secondary education? Powell wondered whether, if *Rodriguez* was upheld, the state of Virginia would be required to spend as much money on every state university as it did on the University of Virginia.

Powell's experience on the Richmond School Board led him to develop great affection for the idea of local control over the schools. He knew firsthand the important and significant work done by local school boards. Of course, similar good work might be done at the state level, but the very notion of this offended his deeper sense of the value of decentralized authority. The problem, however, was to reconcile the civic necessity of education with the problem of unequal funding that clearly existed. Put simply, if education was crucial to the survival and success of the republic, should the quality of education be dependent on the wealth of the district in which a child resided?

On the other hand, was the cure of centralized control worse than the disease of inequality?

## Lessons from Virginia

Powell quickly saw a way out of this dilemma. He did not believe that unequal funding led directly to unequal education. The link between funding and quality had never, to Powell's way of thinking, been definitively made. Furthermore, although some minimal level of education might be necessary to perform basic civic duties such as voting, it was impossible to establish whether the education provided in poor districts was in fact insufficient for such tasks. When it came to the funding of education, deprivation was a relative term. After all, every child had the opportunity to receive some amount of free education.

Moreover, equalized funding might not be the panacea the plaintiffs had anticipated. Powell (and many of the other justices) very quickly agreed with Assistant Attorney General Bailey's conclusion that victory for the Edgewood parents would mean that only absolute equality in per-student funding would satisfy the Equal Protection Clause, despite the fact that Gochman and the parents were not necessarily seeking that remedy. The case as written asked only for a declaration that the current system was unconstitutional and an injunction forcing state officials to remedy the problem. After the decision in *Serrano* was handed down, Gochman was willing to accept the power equalizing approach of Coons, Sugarman, and Clune, which did not guarantee equal funding but only the equal ability of districts to raise money through property taxes.

Although he knew about the Coons team approach, Powell still maintained that upholding the lower court decision would mandate equality in funding. This misunderstanding of the intention in *Rodriguez* led directly to Powell's main criticism: Equalized funding would result in less, not more, money for urban districts. Powell knew from his school board service that many urban districts already received more money per student than some suburban and rural districts. If the Supreme Court mandated equality, therefore, those better-funded districts might well see a cut in per-student funding.

By the end of summer 1972, it was clear Powell had already decided that the district court had erred and he had arrived at an initial approach for attacking the decision. The depositions and expert testimony taken by Gochman, however, would be a problem. In order to combat the data presented to the district court, Powell would need numbers of his own. At the end of August 1972, the justice drafted a letter to J. Harvie Wilkinson, Jr. — father of Powell's law clerk, J. Harvie Wilkinson, III, and one of Powell's oldest and best-connected friends in Richmond — with the subject line "*San Antonio v. Rodriguez.*"

In the text of the letter, Powell made no effort to hide his displeasure with the lower court decision. He complained to Wilkinson about the district court "following almost slavishly . . . *Serrano* . . . which in turn adopted almost literally the 'activist scholarship' theory of Professor Coons and Sugarman in their book *Private Wealth and Public Education.*" His own experience, he wrote, caused him to disagree with the idea of state-controlled education. He then asked Wilkinson to provide him current per-district school funding information from Virginia. He planned to use these numbers to demonstrate to his brethren on the Court that any attempt to mandate equalized funding would result in less money for urban schools — many of which contained large minority populations.

## Bench Memo

Powell had filled the seat on the Court previously occupied by Justice Hugo Black. When Powell took over in January of 1972, he asked two of Black's law clerks, Larry Hammond and William Kelly, to stay on. Hammond and Kelly, along with J. Harvie Wilkinson, III, whom Powell himself recruited, would work with Powell throughout the October 1972 Supreme Court term. As Powell prepared for that session, he decided to assign work on *Rodriguez* to Hammond, and drafted a memo to him regarding the case. Hammond had grown up in Texas and attended the University of Texas Law School. Powell might have presumed that the young man would provide insight into how the Texas system operated. After all, Hammond was a product of the Texas public schools.

{ *Chapter 5* }

In this initial memo, Powell asked that Hammond search for data that compared quality of education with the money spent on education. Any correlation, suggested the justice, was only assumed. A few weeks later Powell drafted two more memos: one to Larry Hammond, and one to J. Harvie Wilkinson, III. Wilkinson, although not specifically assigned to the case, would participate in Powell's chamber deliberations about *Rodriguez*. He was also the most conservative of Powell's clerks, and the justice might have thought that he could rely on Wilkinson to support his own opposition to the district court decision.

Unlike Wilkinson, Larry Hammond was initially sympathetic to the complaints of the Edgewood parents. Indeed, both Hammond and Kelly thought that Powell should vote to uphold the Texas district court. Hammond's assignment from Powell, however, was not to argue for any particular decision, but rather to draft what is known as a "bench memo." A bench memo is used by the justices as part of their preparation to hear oral arguments, and generally summarizes the issues and the legal arguments raised by the controversy. When Powell assigned *Rodriguez* to Hammond, he made clear that it was "of the highest priority."

Hammond presented his bench memo to Powell on Monday, October 2, 1972, the proverbial "first Monday in October" when the Supreme Court begins its session following the summer recess. In the memo, Hammond advised Powell that he had more enthusiasm for *Rodriguez* than he could "recall possessing heretofore for any other cases." The clerk explained that he saw in the case "a rare combination of social, legal, and philosophical considerations." Then, in reviewing the facts issued, he provided Powell with what would evolve into one of the central points of the justice's eventual majority opinion for the Court.

Hammond shared with Powell that he had grown up in the Ysleta School District, then one of the poorer districts in Texas. When it was time for him to go to high school, however, he traveled to the wealthier El Paso School District because Ysleta had no local high school. His point was that his *parents'* wealth or lack thereof was not relevant. Instead, what was important was the wealth of the district. This biographical information illustrated one of the difficulties inherent in Gochman's argument. If *Rodriguez* was a case about wealth discrimination, how would the Court identify with any precision individuals who were victims of unequal treatment? The correlation between individual wealth and district wealth was not perfect, as Hammond's own situation demonstrated.

Hammond proceeded to identify for Powell the primary constitutional questions involved in the case. Since this was an equal protection case, the justices had to determine first which legal test was appropriate. Following *Serrano* and *Van Dusartz*, the three-judge court in *Rodriguez* had identified wealth as a suspect classification, and found that the right to an education was a fundamental constitutional interest. The result was that the lower court had applied strict scrutiny. Hammond concluded that, contrary to the dicta of the district court, if the rational basis test were applied, Texas's funding system would have to be upheld. Therefore, the case appeared to turn, as was often the case, on which legal test was to be applied.

Hammond first addressed the issue of wealth as a suspect classification. He concluded that the school financing system in Texas "[did] discriminate against the property poor." Nevertheless, the precedents relating to wealth as a suspect classification were not at all clear. Hammond pointed to a decision by his former boss, the late Justice Hugo Black. In the 1971 case of *James v. Valtierra*, Black had written a majority opinion rejecting an equal protection challenge to a California constitutional provision requiring a referendum before low-income housing could be built in a community. One of the claims brought by those eligible for such housing was that the referendum requirement discriminated against the poor. Black concluded, however, that discrimination based on wealth, unlike racial classifications, did not trigger the higher level of judicial scrutiny. Hammond was unsure, however, whether *Valtierra* was still a valid precedent, since it had been undercut, although never overturned, by some of the Court's later holdings, especially *Bullock v. Carter* (1972), in which the Court had invalidated a Texas filing fee requirement.

Even if wealth-based classifications were not constitutionally suspect, there was still another path to strict scrutiny. According to precedent, strict scrutiny would be applied when the Court determined that a state action resulted in the deprivation of a fundamental right or interest recognized by the Constitution. These same precedents, however, did not offer a great deal of guidance when it came to determining which interests or rights are properly deemed fundamental.

Hammond reviewed the cases in which the Court had discovered fundamental interests — for example, the right to vote and the right to travel — and tried to link these to education cases such as *Brown v. Board of Education*. One of the difficulties identified by Hammond, however, lay in the fact that the Constitution never speaks directly to the subject of education, and states are not commanded to set up a system of public education. Also, there was no absolute deprivation of an interest involved in this complaint. Only the relative quality of the schools, not the existence of schools, was in question.

All of these precedents led Hammond to argue that Powell might want to consider an intermediate legal test that would allow the Court to demand more than a rational basis for the system but less than a compelling state interest. The level of scrutiny afforded to the state's actions would be linked to the Court's conclusions about the importance of education in the U.S. constitutional system. Powell could then decide the case based on how important education was thought to be on a "sliding scale of values." Hammond ended his memo by proposing several remedies Powell might be able to support, and included a reference to "power equalization."

Powell did not initially respond to the memo, but instead decided to jot down some of his own thoughts. Since the prior spring, the parties to the case as well as various amicus curie had been submitting briefs to the Court. From what Powell had read, he concluded that there was the real possibility that affirming the lower court in *Rodriguez* could lead to federal control of the schools. This clearly worried him.

For Powell, the racial element in the case was a "red herring" — that is, an element that distracted from the real issues in the case. In his estimation, *Rodriguez* was not about racial discrimination. He was convinced that, in Richmond for example, blacks would be hurt by equal funding, possibly receiving less money per student. As a practical matter, he knew from his years on the Virginia School Board that the state could not afford to fund every school at the same level as, say, a wealthy district like Arlington. Finally, his notes indicate that he agreed with Larry Hammond's point that there was a difference between absolute and relative deprivation of a fundamental right.

As he worked through the case, Powell seemed convinced that others on the Court would share his perspective if only they were aware of actual funding situations within the states. Unfortunately, his friend J. Harvie Wilkinson, Jr., still had not responded to his early request for the relevant numbers from Virginia. In frustration, Powell penned a second letter to Wilkinson, suggesting that his friend call the state treasurer to request the data. Powell cautioned Wilkinson, however, not to mention Powell's name or any specific case.

The case continued to weigh heavily on Powell's mind and he spent many hours reviewing Larry Hammond's bench memo. Oral argument in the case was scheduled for the next week, and Powell wanted to be prepared. Finally, on October 12, a letter arrived from Virginia. It was from another Richmond associate and friend, H. I. Willet. Willet had sent an unreleased copy of a document entitled "Report of the Sub-Committee to the School Division Criteria Study Commission." Willet had chaired the subcommittee that drafted the study. The report noted that "it [was] not yet possible to evaluate the impact of the *Serrano v. Priest* and *Rodriguez v. San Antonio* class action suits on the organizational patterns of public education." At the end of the report was an addendum containing the per-pupil spending figures Powell sought from Wilkinson. He underlined the numbers for the Arlington County and Richmond School Districts and prepared to hear oral arguments.

# Briefs

During the Texas phase of the case, Gochman had faced off against Pat Bailey, an assistant attorney general for the state, who was skilled at appellate argument. In February 1972 Bailey had argued before the Supreme Court on behalf of Texas in the case of *Jefferson v. Hackney* (Justice Rehnquist cited this case during oral argument in *Rodriguez*). *Rodriguez* had quickly evolved into a case with serious national implications. If the three-judge district court decision in *Rodriguez* were upheld by the Supreme Court, the school financing systems in nearly every state would have to be changed. This was not the first time such a precedent-setting case had come from Texas; as in those prior cases, Texas Attorney General Crawford Martin knew just where to turn. He called on one of Mark Yudof's colleagues at the University of Texas Law School: Charles Alan Wright.

## Charles Alan Wright

It would not be an exaggeration to say that, for the Supreme Court battle over *Rodriguez*, Texas had brought in the biggest of the big guns. Although only in his mid-forties, Wright had already developed a stellar reputation both as an academic and as an advocate before the Supreme Court. Throughout his career, he would argue thirteen cases before the nation's High Court, losing only three times. By the time he took over *Rodriguez*, he had already appeared eight times before the Court, representing Texas in such landmark cases as *Texas v. Mitchell* (a companion case to *Oregon v. Mitchell*, which involved the right of eighteen-year-olds to vote) and *Furman v. Georgia* (the 1972 case that struck down the death penalty). For a time, Wright was counsel for President Richard Nixon in the Watergate matter. His acumen was quickly evident when, on July 21, 1972, the State of Texas submitted its brief in *Rodriguez.*

---

## Appellant's Brief

Before oral arguments are heard by the Supreme Court, the parties to the case, known as the appellants and appellees, file legal briefs, which are essentially written arguments from both sides laying out the facts of the case and explaining to the Court why it should reach a particular decision. These main briefs are supplemented in most modern cases by *amicus curiae* or "friend of the court" briefs filed by groups or individuals who have an interest in the outcome of the case but are not direct parties. In *Rodriguez,* for example, an amici brief (plural for amicus) was filed jointly by the governors of Minnesota, Wisconsin, Maine, South Dakota, and Michigan along with the attorney general of New Jersey. This brief argued that the lower court decision ought to be overturned. At the same time, the mayor of Baltimore, Maryland, teamed up with the AFL-CIO, the National Urban League, and the Texas League of Women Voters to urge that the three-judge district court decision be upheld. The Republic National Bank of Dallas worked together with the First City National Bank of Houston, Mercantile National Bank at Dallas, and the Bank of Texas to draft an amici brief to assert that, whatever the outcome in the Supreme Court, the resulting judgment "should not affect the enforceability of Texas school district bonds."

Amicus briefs are important, often making bold arguments that the main parties avoid for fear of overreaching with the Court. Still, the most important briefs remain those filed by the actual parties to a case. Since Texas had lost in the lower court, it would be responsible for appealing to the Supreme Court; hence, its brief was the "appellant's brief." Although there are seven names listed on the appellant's brief in *Rodriguez,* the document bears the clear imprint of Charles Alan Wright, the attorney who would eventually argue the case before the Court.

Wright was known as one of his generation's preeminent "legal realists." Legal realism as a theory of judicial decisionmaking arose in the early twentieth century in reaction to more mechanistic theories then popular among the nation's legal elites. Legal realism took issue with the notion that judges were mere automatons, neatly matching the law with the facts to reach predetermined conclusions. More "realistic" legal theorists recognized that judges often exercise considerable discretion when deciding cases. As Walter Murphy, C. Herman Pritchett, and Lee Epstein have explained, legal realism referred to "several varieties of jurisprudence and was more a state of mind than a concerted movement." The one point upon which all legal realists could agree was that legal precedents (decisions rendered by earlier courts addressing a similar issue) rarely, if ever, pointed toward a single outcome, and therefore it might be as important — indeed, more important — to argue the facts of a case as it was to point judges toward favorable precedents. This was precisely the tactic Wright employed in *Rodriguez*.

Altogether, the appellant's brief was forty-seven pages long, with the actual argument beginning on page six. Wright did not even refer to a relevant legal precedent until page twenty-five. Here is how he summarized his approach: "[A]fter stating the nature of the problem and of the critics' argument directed to it, we will consider the unsound factual assumptions on which that argument is based, the fatal weakness of the legal analysis offered in its support, and the dangerous consequences that would follow if it were to be read into the Constitution." The legal analysis was sandwiched between discussions of facts and consequences.

Wright wrote that if "fiscal neutrality" were really demanded by the Fourteenth Amendment, then there were only two options available to Texas and the forty-eight other states sharing its approach to school finance: Either they would have to adopt statewide systems of school finance, eliminating local funding altogether, or they could adopt the "power equalizing" model provided in "the engaging and provocative book by Professors John E. Coons, William Clune, III, and Stephen D. Sugarman." The problem with power equalizing, Wright argued, was that it assumed money and quality went hand-in-hand. Allowing that "some minimum sum of dollars" might be necessary, he explained that equalized funding for schools did not mean an equalized quality of education for students. The notion that funding and quality were related was, asserted Wright, an assumption rather than a demonstrated fact, and it was not "the custom of courts to let assumption substitute for proof when they are asked to decide great issues."

But Wright was not through with power equalizing. For his brief goes on to note that Proposition 1 (the other name for district power equalizing) was based on a second assumption: the relationship between individual and district wealth. Here Wright's target was the data presented in Professor Berke's affidavit to *Rodriguez* (see Table 6.1).

The problem was obvious. The median family income in districts where the property value was only $10,000 to $30,000 per student was higher than it was in districts where the per-student property values were more than three times as high. This table also showed that the relationship established between wealth and race in *Hobson* (although Hobson was not specifically cited) was sketchy at best. If one eliminated the ten richest and four poorest districts, there was virtually no relationship.

The appellant's brief then moved on to confront the primary legal argument made by Gochman and accepted by the three-judge district court in Texas. Recall that the district court, following *Serrano* and *Van Dusartz*, had declared wealth to be a suspect classification and education to be a fundamental right. Both conclusions led to the same result, the application of strict scrutiny. Under this test, unless Texas could show that it had a compelling state interest in maintaining its funding system, the laws establishing that system would have to be found in violation of the Equal Protection Clause of the Fourteenth Amendment.

Table 6.1  District wealth, income, race, and school revenues

| Market Value of Taxable Property Per Student | Median Family Income from 1960 | Percent Minority Student | State and Local Revenues Per Student |
|---|---|---|---|
| Above $100,000 (10 Districts) | $5,900 | 8 | $815 |
| $100,000–$50,000 (26 Districts) | $4,425 | 32 | $544 |
| $50,000–$30,000 (30 Districts) | $4,900 | 23 | $483 |
| $30,000–$10,000 (40 Districts) | $5,050 | 31 | $462 |
| Below $10,000 (4 Districts) | $3,325 | 79 | $305 |

{ *Chapter 6* }

Wright had obviously decided to combat the very foundations of the application of this legal test. He began with the question of whether *Brown v. Board of Education* (1954) had established education as a fundamental right. To answer this question, Wright relied on a two-page quote from a decision that Judge Alexander Harvey, II, had rendered on behalf of the district court in Maryland in *Parker v. Mandel* (1972), in which he had reviewed the relevant Supreme Court cases and concluded that the right to vote, the right to a fair trial, and the right to travel had been deemed fundamental interests to be tested under the higher standard. Harvey's opinion went on to say that classifications based on race or ethnic background were also grounds for strict scrutiny. Harvey asserted that "The strict scrutiny test was applied in *Brown* not because education [was] a fundamental interest but because classification by race [was] clearly suspect."

To address the claim that socioeconomic status was a suspect classification, Wright used a quote from a more recent Supreme Court case, *Jefferson v. Hackney* (1972), argued by another of the brief's authors, Pat Bailey, which involved the allocation of welfare benefits. Justice Rehnquist, writing for the majority in that case, had noted that "the problems of the poor and the needy are not subject to a constitutional straitjacket." Wright took this to mean that classifications based on wealth should not trigger strict scrutiny.

Both sides in *Rodriguez* recognized that the vote on the Court would be very close, and that Justice Powell would probably serve as the swing vote. Mark Yudof recalled that this closeness led those representing the Edgewood parents to try to tailor their arguments to the new justice from Virginia. It is not clear whether Wright did the same. Near the end of the appellant's brief, however, he presented evidence that matched up exactly with Powell's way of thinking. Gochman's star witness, Joel Berke, was again targeted.

In addition to providing a deposition for the plaintiffs in *Rodriguez*, Berke had served as a consultant to the Senate Select Committee on Equal Educational Opportunity. "Some of the huzzahs that have greeted the opinion below . . . have been from those who are concerned about the problems of city schools and who have seen in Proposition 1 a device that will funnel vast new sums into those schools," the brief observed, calling the conclusion "almost certainly an illusion." Professor Berke had prepared a report in support of Proposition 1 for the Senate Select Committee in which he wrote: "finance reform of the type just described [he had cited *Serrano, Van Dusartz*, and the three-judge district court decision in *Rodriguez*] . . . may well exacerbate the problems of a substantial portion of urban schools." The reason was that many urban areas already had a high tax base because of an abundance of taxable commercial property. Whether this quotation from Berke merely echoed Powell's way of thinking about the case, or was in fact the impetus for Justice Powell's letters to his friend J. Harvie Wilkinson, Jr., asking for school funding numbers from Virginia, is unclear. What is clear, however, is that this was an argument that was very important to Powell.

---

## Appellee's Brief

The title of this case, *San Antonio v. Rodriguez*, is confusing because by the time the case got to the Supreme Court, the San Antonio Independent School District had essentially switched sides. Having been dismissed from the case by Judge Spears, the school district later offered an amicus curiae brief in support of the Edgewood parents' position. Since the parents had won in the lower court, they were considered the appellees at the Supreme Court, defending their victory against the appeal by the State of Texas. There were, in all, five names on the appellee's brief, including Arthur Gochman, Mark Yudof, Warren Weir, Manuel Montez, and, as a last minute concession to MALDEF, Mario Obledo, one of that group's founders.

The appellee's brief was filed on August 21, 1972, about a month after Wright's appellant's brief was delivered to the Court, and it followed very closely the lines of the Texas brief. It was a measure of the importance of *Serrano* that Wright's brief focused not at all on *Hobson* (in fact, it is not even listed in the "Table of Authorities" in the appellant's brief), but on the power equalizing approach championed by the Coons team. Curiously enough, and perhaps in no small way because of Mark Yudof's role in crafting the document, this omission was carried forward into the brief for the Edgewood parents. Indeed, given how important *Hobson* was to Gochman as *Rodriguez* began, the fact that the Washington, D.C., case was omitted from his Supreme Court brief was striking. In addition to tracking Wright's legal precedents, Gochman and

Yudof did not stray very far from the Texas brief's emphasis on the facts before the Court. They clearly felt that if the case were to be argued based upon what was actually happening in Texas, the appellees had a distinct advantage. The data were on their side.

After reviewing the facts of the case and emphasizing the failure of the Texas legislature to act in response to Judge Spears's postponement of the case, the appellee's brief moved to the alleged basis of the Edgewood parents' complaint. In the appellant's brief, Wright had offered evidence that there was no correlation between district wealth and individual wealth. Rather than directly taking on this claim, Gochman and Yudof offered evidence from Professor Berke's affidavit (see Table 6.2).

This table was said to illustrate two propositions. First, the table showed that there was "an almost perfect correlation between the size of the tax base and the amount of educational dollars expended per child." The table also indicated that the poorer districts were taxing themselves at higher rates than the wealthier districts. The point was that it was impossible for the poorest districts to tax themselves out of their financial condition. The state's Minimal Foundation Program did not help because the amount of money guaranteed to a district was calculated based in part on the education and experience of the teachers employed by the local schools. Wealthier districts, with their ability to raise more money per student, were able to hire more experienced and better educated teachers. This, in turn, qualified the districts for a larger foundation amount. The result was that a lack of district wealth translated into a lower quality of education (at least as measured by teacher qualifications), and this situation, the brief explained, was actually exacerbated by the foundation program.

The brief then moved to a discussion of the legal issues involved in the case. Gochman's position had always been that Texas should lose regardless of which of the two legal tests — rational basis or strict scrutiny — was used by the Court. In his brief, he argued that "even where the compelling state interest test [strict scrutiny] is held inapplicable, it does not follow that any state interest, however attenuated and insignificantly related to the object of the legislation automatically passes constitutional muster."

Nevertheless, the brief maintained that the proper test was strict scrutiny. The required triggers for that test were, as the three-judge court had recognized, that either a fundamental constitutional right

Table 6.2  District wealth, family income, race, and school revenues

| Market Value of Taxable Property Per Student | Median Family Income | Percent Minority Students | Equalized Tax Rates on $100 | Local Revenues Per Student | State Revenues Per Student | State and Local Revenues Per Student |
|---|---|---|---|---|---|---|
| Above $100,000 (10 Districts) | $5,900 | 8% | $0.31 | $610 | $205 | $815 |
| $100,000–$50,000 (26 Districts) | $4,425 | 32% | $0.38 | $287 | $257 | $544 |
| $50,000–$30,000 (30 Districts) | $4,900 | 23% | $0.55 | $224 | $260 | $484 |
| $30,000–$10,000 (40 Districts) | $5,050 | 31% | $0.72 | $166 | $295 | $461 |
| Below $10,000 (4 Districts) | $3,325 | 79% | $0.70 | $63 | $243 | $305 |

was abridged, or that a suspect classification had resulted from some state action. Here, the brief insisted, both elements were present. As might have been expected, in support of a fundamental constitutional interest in education, the brief quoted Chief Justice Warren's opinion in *Brown v. Board of Education* (1954), in which he had written that education was "perhaps the most important function of state and local governments." Gochman and Yudof had anticipated possible objections to this argument, including the fact that the Court had recently failed to recognize similar interests, including the interest that the poor had in receiving welfare benefits, as being fundamental. The most important and recent case to make this argument was *Jefferson v. Hackney* (1972), in which the Supreme Court (at Pat Bailey's urging) had rejected a challenge to a Texas decision to lower payments made under the Aid to Families with Dependent Children (AFDC) program.

In their brief, Gochman and Yudof pointed out that education, unlike the welfare payments at issue in *Hackney*, is a state service that has a long history, being called for in every state constitution throughout the country. Moreover, students were compelled to go to school. The state thereby had created for itself a more direct obligation to provide this traditional and required benefit on an equal basis. Moreover, the brief held, welfare payments had "historically received less judicial solicitude than education."

In the next section of the brief, the appellees drew an additional and important link between education and the right to political participation. "[O]nly a well-educated, articulate citizen," they argued, "is in a position to make himself heard by government." The conclusion was that "by assuring children in poor districts an inferior educational opportunity, the State of Texas [had] greatly disadvantaged these children in their ability to participate in the democratic process."

Having attempted to establish that education was a fundamental constitutional right (or interest), it was time to move to the argument that wealth was a suspect classification. Here, Gochman exhibited just how far he had moved from an earlier *Hobson*-based approach to the case. Early in the appellee's brief, Berke's data had been reproduced, suggesting a link between the percentage of Mexican Americans in a district and the amount of money available per student. The problem with using this data, however, was that there had not been any legislated segregation of Mexican Americans in Texas. Although Richard Avena, director of the

Southwestern Field Office of the U.S. Commission on Civil Rights and one of Gochman's witnesses, had offered testimony that the state had sponsored segregation through its enforcement of restrictive covenants in property deeds, this was one step away from claiming de jure segregation. Therefore, any legal argument that relied on race would have to overcome the hurdle of appearing, on its face, to be asking the Court to remedy the effects not of de jure, but of de facto, segregation. Yudof was convinced that the Court would not go in this direction. Therefore, he tried to steer Gochman toward the approach taken by the plaintiffs in *Serrano*, emphasizing that wealth alone, even absent race, was either a suspect classification or, and this might have proved important, ought to be subject to an inquiry more searching than that ordinarily demanded by the rational basis test.

In his brief for the appellants, Wright had tried to anticipate this argument by arguing that the Court's decision in *James v. Valtierra* (1971) already disposed of this line of attack. As discussed in Chapter 5, *Valtierra* was a case out of California where discrimination against the poor had been alleged, and where the Court had rejected a strict scrutiny approach. But as Lewis Powell's clerk Larry Hammond had observed in a memo to the justice, *Valtierra* was arguably contradicted by *Bullock v. Carter* (1972). *Bullock* was a challenge to a Texas law that required a substantial filing fee to be paid by candidates seeking to have their name placed on a ballot in that state. This law was found to discriminate against those who were too poor to pay the fee, and the Court used a version of the strict scrutiny standard to overturn the requirement. Gochman and Yudof therefore had a potential precedent, and wisely relied on *Bullock* in claiming that the Court now recognized wealth as a suspect classification. They also, however, tried to convince the Court that even if rational basis review was the standard applied, it need not be considered a mere rubber stamp upon whatever the state had decided to do. Their authority for this was a 1972 case, *Aetna v. Weber Casualty and Surety Company*. In that case the Court had stated that, under the Equal Protection Clause, what was required, "at a minimum, [was] that a statutory classification bear some rational relationship to a legitimate state purpose." That opinion, the authors of the appellee's brief pointed out, was written by "Mr. Justice Powell." Indeed, as the case moved to oral argument stage, Powell increasingly became the focus of both sides in *Rodriguez*.

# Oral Arguments

Arguments before the Supreme Court in cases to which the justices have agreed to grant a full hearing consist of two related parts. The written briefs are obviously important and represent an opportunity for counsel on both sides to present their position in succinct and organized fashion, complete with footnotes and citations explaining the relevant precedents. Following the submission of briefs is an event referred to as oral argument. According to the Supreme Court's official rules, "Oral argument should emphasize and clarify the written arguments in the briefs on the merits."

Grounded in tradition, the influence of oral argument on the outcome of a case is the subject of dispute among both Court scholars and the justices themselves. During oral argument, the attorneys are given the chance, in the words of the late Chief Justice Rehnquist, "to confront face to face the nine Members of the Court who will ponder and decide [their] case."

Oral argument also gives the justices an opportunity to argue publicly with each other. Through their questioning of opposing counsels, the justices may try to influence the views of their colleagues prior to conference. If this was to happen in *Rodriguez*, however, Gochman faced at least a minor obstacle. For at 11:43 A.M. on Thursday, October 12, 1972, when Chief Justice Warren Burger announced that oral argument would begin in the case of *San Antonio v. Rodriguez*, not all of the justices were present. Indeed, the jurist that Gochman had every reason to believe would be the most sympathetic to his argument, Thurgood Marshall, was absent due to an illness. Although Gochman was virtually assured of Marshall's vote when the case was handed down, he might have benefited from the former civil rights leader's questions at oral argument. After all, part of Gochman's argument rested on principles first announced by the Court in *Brown v.*

*Board of Education* (1954), a case argued by Marshall himself and a decision intimately connected to the success of the NAACP Legal Defense and Education Fund.

---

## Wright's Argument

Charles Wright was the first to step up to the podium in *Rodriguez*. If Gochman had hoped to avoid the case devolving into an argument about Proposition 1, he was quickly disappointed. In a calm, matter-of-fact manner, Wright began by quoting from Coons, Sugarman, and Clune. In the quote, the authors had talked about how little was understood about the "goals and methods" of education, and therefore counseled the value of "local variety, experimentation, and independence" in this area. Wright argued that this "local variety" was precisely what the State of Texas was trying to preserve, and provided the "rational basis" for the state's funding system. The tactic was obvious: Wright was trying to show that the inventors of the remedy adopted by the three-judge district court did not fully understand the implications of their approach. They were attempting to "impose a constitutional straightjacket" (a nod to Justice Rehnquist's opinion in *Jefferson v. Hackney* [1972]) on local control of schools, although admitting they did not know much about how to provide quality education.

Wright then backtracked a bit and admitted that district power equalizing actually did allow for some local variation. Nevertheless, argued Wright, this point merely emphasized both how little was known about how district power equalizing would work in practice, and might even suggest that the approach, rather than relieving a constitutional infirmity, would itself result in a violation of the Equal Protection Clause. After all, tax rates would still be set by residents within local school districts, and therefore the actual money spent on a child's education would be dependent on, in Wright's words, what the child's "friends and neighbors" thought appropriate.

If Wright had sought to gain Justice Powell's attention as a potential swing vote, he had succeeded. Indeed, the justice did not need to be coaxed, since he already considered the case very important and had spent much time considering the outcome, even writing several letters commenting on the case and requesting information that might be helpful in rendering a judgment. As was his style during oral argument, Powell took careful notes. Wright's critique of the constitutionality of district power equalizing clearly had interested him, and he had tried to transcribe for himself what the attorney said. He wrote: "D.P.E. [district power equalizing] may be [unconstitutional] as it results in the input for education of some children being dependent in part on what taxpayers of *other* districts are willing to pay [emphasis is in original]."

Powell — probably inadvertently since these notes were only for his use — had made a key error in this transcription. Wright had never used the word "other." In fact, the word makes no sense here, since the variation would be caused by the voters within a child's own district. Voters in other districts do not determine the tax rates of others, and district power equalizing only calls for an equal yield at given tax rate. Why did Justice Powell make this mistake? From the start, Powell had thought that *Rodriguez* was about a state takeover of education. This concern only made sense, however, if control over local educational decisions was done by "others" outside of the local district. Powell, therefore, changed Wright's words to make them consistent with his own theory of the case.

The first question Wright faced came from Justice Byron White. White challenged the assertion that district power equalizing would necessarily lead to more inequality in Texas. He pointed out that under the system then in place, it was "impossible for some districts to have a sufficient input." Wright countered that the state's Minimal Foundation Program guaranteed that what was needed would be provided. When Justice White pressed him on this, asking whether he was claiming that the foundation program was itself a form of district power equalizing, Wright answered in the negative and pointedly replied that he did not think that the district power equalizing program called for in Proposition 1 was in "the small print of the Fourteenth Amendment."

Justice White wanted to continue down this path and asked several questions about whether the foundation program really guaranteed adequacy. Wright answered that, as he understood the Edgewood parents' claim, the case was about relative inequality, not adequacy — although he conceded that some level of adequacy might be required by the Constitution. This line of questioning was interrupted by Justice Rehnquist.

Like Powell, Rehnquist had only recently been named to the Court. Unlike Powell, Rehnquist was aggressively conservative in his outlook on the Constitution. Responding to Wright's concession about the possibility of the Constitution requiring an adequate education be provided, Justice Rehnquist wanted to know whether a state could "just get out of public education." The implication was that any discussion of adequacy was really outside of the Constitution, since the document could not logically speak of a minimum amount of a good not required to be provided.

Wright assumed that the case Justice Rehnquist relied upon for this conclusion was *Griffin v. Prince Edward County* (1964), a case involving the constitutionality of closing all the public schools in a Virginia county. In *Prince Edward County*, the Court had invalidated the school closings based on the finding that the action was clearly in response to efforts to desegregate the schools. Nevertheless, Justice Black's majority opinion in that case seemed to suggest that the public schools might be closed, but only for reasons not involving racial discrimination. Given Wright's encyclopedic knowledge of legal history, he may have known that he was treading on rather risky ground when he answered Justice Rehnquist, since Justice Powell had been one of the leaders of the efforts to reopen the Virginia schools. Whatever the reason, Wright was clearly nervous about traveling down this path, and even suggested that it might run into problems under the First Amendment.

Wright showed his experience as a litigator before the Court, nimbly using a question from Justice Brennan about whether a state would have to implement statewide assessment of property value in order to fairly impose district power equalization, to move back to his prepared comments. Questions about how to finance education, like questions about the disposition of welfare payments posed, were, in the words of Wright, "intractable." He explained that cases such as *Jefferson v. Hackney* demonstrated that the Court would not "impose a constitutional straightjacket on the states." This was why, Wright continued, in cases like *Rodriguez*, the proper legal test was rational basis, a standard that allowed for legislative flexibility. The fundamental rights approach to invoking strict scrutiny would not work, he argued, because, based on existing precedent, it would require the Court to conclude that "the educational needs of the poor are fundamental, while their needs for food, for housing, are not."

The Court then took a break for lunch. After the justices returned, Wright resumed his argument. He began this time by criticizing the three-judge district court in Texas for having made "the implicit assumption that in education, money is quality." Once again, Wright had expressed an opinion already held by Justice Powell, and Powell began to take careful notes. He wrote, again underlining for emphasis, that the "D.C. [District Court] *assumed* that *money* equals *quality*" [emphasis in original]. Justice Powell kept writing as Wright attacked a more explicit conclusion reached by the lower court that there was "a correlation between poor people and poor districts." He pointed out the problem with the tables Berke had provided in his affidavit, in which a relationship could only be found at the extreme ends of the wealth scale. Wright then cited a *Yale Law Journal* study that had been published just two days earlier. The study had examined Connecticut school districts and found an inverse relationship between the wealth of a district and the amount spent on education. Justice Powell copied down the *Yale Law Journal* page numbers in his notes.

At this point Justice Douglas stopped Wright, saying, "As I read this record, Mr. Wright, it seemed to me that the testimony . . . pretty clearly demonstrated there is an unequal treatment of these respondents who are Americans of Spanish ancestry at educational levels. Is that any part of the litigation?" Perhaps owing to the absence of Justice Marshall from the bench that day, this was one of the few times during the hearing that race or ethnicity was specifically mentioned by one of the justices. Wright quickly dispensed with the question, explaining that the relationship between the wealth of a district and its racial makeup — a crucial fact in Judge J. Skelly Wright's opinion in *Hobson* — was merely "a happenstance" that was not replicated throughout the State of Texas.

---

## Gochman's Reply

It was now time for Arthur Gochman to step up to the podium. Unlike Wright, the Texas lawyer had never argued before the Supreme Court and he did not have the law professor's apparent ease before the justices. With a slightly monotone delivery broken only slightly by his pronounced Texas accent, he began reading from an obviously prepared text. He quoted the lower court's opinion, in which the three-judge panel had written: "Those districts most rich in property also have the highest median family income and the lowest percentage of minority students; while the poorer districts are poorer in income and predominantly minority in composition." He reminded the justices that the lower court had found that the State of Texas failed *both* the strict scrutiny and the rational basis standard, and stated that the Supreme Court had to decide in this case whether to "approve district wealth as a proper basis for distributing public school education."

Like Justice Powell, Gochman had been listening carefully to Wright's argument and was prepared to respond to each of the charges made by him. Gochman began by addressing Justice Brennan's concern about variations in the assessment of property among the various school districts in Texas. He rephrased the question so that it was about tax rates, rather than the percentage of value assessed; this allowed him to point out that, in Texas, there was a reverse relationship between the rate at which a district was willing to tax itself and the amount raised per student.

Then Justice Blackmun began the questioning. Like the chief justice, Blackmun was from Minnesota. He reflected on his own experience in his home state, pointing out that there was not always a perfect relationship between district wealth and family income. He referred to the Iron Range, an area in Northeastern Minnesota famous for its iron ore mines. As Blackmun recalled the situation, although income was low among the mining families, the districts had the best-funded schools, "the ones with the swimming pools and the tennis courts . . . and the highest paid teachers." Although Gochman interrupted the justice before he could explain, the apparent reason for this was the high amount of tax revenue generated from commercial property. Gochman said that this was not generally the situation in Texas, where "at the top and the bottom, the richest districts have the least poor people and the least minorities; and the poorest districts have the most poor people and the most minorities." Justice Rehnquist, who was obviously familiar with Gochman's data, quickly shot back with a question that was more of a statement: "It [the relationship between district wealth and individual wealth] does not hold true in the middle, does it, at least not by one of your exhibits?" Justice Rehnquist was referring to Berke's data (Table 6.1), which showed an inverse relationship in the middle ranges, with slightly wealthier people living in poorer districts.

Gochman tried to direct the Court to data included in his brief that showed a perfect correlation between family income and property value per student in Bexar County, but was interrupted by Chief Justice Burger. The chief justice wanted to know why the logic of Gochman's argument would not extend across state lines. Notwithstanding the limitations of the Fourteenth Amendment (which speaks to states), why, Burger wanted to know, should one state have better schools than another? When Gochman conceded that this might be true "as a moral proposition," Burger revealed disdain for the position, suggesting that the Texas attorney's "argument would apply with equal force whether you call it 'moral grounds' or 'totalitarian philosophy.'" The chief justice continued to attack Gochman's position, asking how education might rate in importance alongside "the need for police protection, fire protection, public health facilities."

If Burger hoped to batter Gochman into some concessions, his line of argument had just the opposite effect. For the first time during the oral argument, Gochman became less formal in his delivery, and a hint of anger could be heard in his voice. Gochman explained that, unlike the other services Burger had mentioned in his question, "education affects matters guaranteed by the Bill of Rights." As examples, he cited the right to vote, the right to free speech, and even the right to serve on a jury, since those who cannot "read, write, understand, and speak the English language" were barred from serving on federal juries.

Chief Justice Burger was not willing to let this point go and next asked Gochman to address how an individual's constitutional interest in education might be more important than the interest in health care facilities. Gochman took the question as an opportunity to illustrate his main argument in favor of a fundamental constitutional interest in education: "Public health, food, lodging, those things are of great economic importance," admitted Gochman, "but they are not matters that are related to those things guaranteed by the Bill of Rights." Although it is not likely that Gochman could have picked up on this, his argument about the relationship between education and other constitutional guarantees seemed to intrigue Justice Powell, and for the first time since the Texas lawyer had started talking, Powell started taking notes without any editorial comments.

Justice White was next to question Gochman. He wanted to return to a question he had first asked Wright. White asked whether *Rodriguez* was a case about adequacy or equality in education. If it was about adequacy, White wanted to know, was Gochman saying that the Texas Minimal Foundation Program did not provide enough money to guarantee that every student received at least a minimal level of education? Gochman agreed that this was true, but claimed it was irrelevant. "Once the State provides the service [education], it has to provide it all on equal terms." Now Gochman was in some trouble, because district power equalizing, as Wright had already explained, would not guarantee equality. If one district chose to tax itself at a lower level than another, its schools would receive less money. When Justice White offered a hypothetical scenario in which one district decided to spend $500 per pupil, and another spent $800 per pupil, Gochman was forced to defend his position by claiming that he "was not preaching for power equalizing," although he admitted that this inequality of spending would probably be constitutional. This led Justice White to return to his original question about whether there was some minimum level of funding that still might be required. When Gochman answered "No, I cannot say that there is any such thing as a minimum," the justice expressed some confusion about the appellee's position.

Justice Rehnquist did not want to let the matter rest, and pointed out similarities between Gochman's argument and the hypothetical scenario proposed by Justice White. Gochman asserted that the situation in Edgewood was different, because it was nearly impossible for Mexican Americans in Edgewood to relocate to a district that was not only willing but able to provide more money for schools. Rehnquist countered by asking for a principle that would allow the Court to distinguish between the two situations. Justice White tried to help, explaining that he understood Gochman's position to be that the equal protection violation had arisen because "some districts are locked in" to their situation of having to settle for less funding.

Finally Justice Powell spoke. He wanted to know if district power equalizing would not produce the same situation, with the same disparities. Gochman suggested that the variances between districts in Texas were so wide under the present system that he could not imagine any system that might be worse. Still, Gochman was forced into the position of admitting that his argument would be satisfied if Edgewood were able (through, for example, the statewide implementation of district power equalization) to choose to get out of its present situation, whether or not it decided to exercise that option. Justice Rehnquist pointed out to Gochman that his "theory" might "leave the students utterly unequal."

Then Rehnquist moved back to the question of discrimination. Justice Douglas had earlier asked Wright whether race was a factor in *Rodriguez*, and Rehnquist wanted to know whether Gochman thought that it was the intention of the State of Texas to discriminate against minorities when it established its school finance system. Gochman's response was cryptic, perhaps reflecting his own ambiguity about making race an issue in the case: "I contend," stated Gochman, " that objectively Texas did what it did — and it could have done something else — and what it did discriminates against minorities." When Rehnquist countered that the Court had, in *Jefferson v. Hackney*, already upheld the Texas welfare program, even though it had similar unintended adverse effect on minority groups, Gochman once again raised the distinction between welfare and education. He also explained that, in the case of school district poverty, the state bore more responsibility since it had set up the rules governing the creation of those districts. As Gochman put it, "the State made [those] districts poor."

After Gochman completed his argument by reminding the Court that the defendant in the original action, the San Antonio Independent School District, had filed an amicus brief in favor of the lower court decision, it was time for Wright to return to the stand for his rebuttal. Wright had six minutes to make his argument, but he used only about half of his time.

## Wright's Rebuttal

Wright began, as he had in his opening statement, by quoting the work of Coons, Sugarman, and Clune. Justice Douglas's earlier question about the possible racial element in *Rodriguez*, along with Gochman's assertion during his turn before the Court that the Texas finance system discriminated against a minority group, raised the possibility that the Supreme Court might reach beyond the lower court reasoning and decide that race was, after all, a factor in this case. This would have led to the application of the strict scrutiny test, and Wright would have been under no illusion that the State of Texas would be able to satisfy that rigorous standard.

The quote from Coons and his colleagues used by Wright stated bluntly that since most of the poor districts are white, "there is no reason to suppose that the system of district-based finance embodies racial bias." This argument was problematic because it was based on data from the State of California, not Texas. Justice Rehnquist immediately criticized Wright on this point, claiming that if he were in Gochman's position, he "would feel rather strongly . . . entitled to stand on the record made in Texas." Wright quickly abandoned this line of argument, but he was not willing to let go of the Coons team's research. In closing, in a way that would later be echoed in Justice Powell's majority opinion, he spoke of his admiration for "the creative scholarship of Professor Coons and his associates, and my colleague Professor Yudof," who, along with Arthur Gochman, had "opened the eyes of the whole country to a very serious problem." The only difference between the two sides, concluded Wright, was "whether a new system should be adopted because this Court finds that the Constitution requires it, or whether we look to legislatures to provide remedies."

---

## Conference

Unlike the other branches of government, the judicial branch is often shielded from the eyes of the public. This is particularly true when it comes to the U.S. Supreme Court. Although reporters and the general public (but no cameras) are allowed to attend oral argument sessions, the rest of the Court's deliberations take place behind closed doors. Although the justices' clerks participate in drafting opinions and in discussions with the justices about the merits of cases, only the nine justices attend the conference at which initial positions are discussed, and no transcripts are kept. Fortunately for students of the Court, the justices themselves take notes. Several years after the justices leave the Court, they sometimes donate their records to libraries and archives. In the case of *San Antonio v. Rodriguez*, the notes of all but two of the justices (Stevens and Rehnquist) who participated are at least partially available. Therefore, it is possible to reconstruct what went on during the conference. The account of the Supreme Court conference in *Rodriguez* that follows relies primarily on the notes of Justices Powell and Douglas.

Five days after oral argument, on Thursday, October 17, 1972, the justices met to discuss *Rodriguez*. By tradition, the chief justice speaks first at conference. As might have been expected, given the hostility he had shown to *Hobson* while still on the court of appeals, Chief Justice Warren Burger was not sympathetic to Gochman's argument. This was evident from the editorial comments he made while reviewing the facts of the case. The central problem of the case, according to Burger, was that property taxes did not raise a consistent amount of revenue for the schools. The lower court in Texas had found that this variation violated the Equal Protection Clause. Burger, however, thought the three-judge court had not been clear as to how this violation had occurred. Instead, Burger argued that the district court had gone along with the thesis of the Coons team, insisting that education not be a function of the wealth of a district. The problem with this approach, explained the chief justice, was that it confused "equal advantage with equal protection." Moreover, Burger had trouble agreeing with the proposition that an individual's constitutional interest in education somehow outranked other interests that might be thought of as equally important. Nevertheless, Burger ended his summary with an interesting confession: He claimed that he would support a constitutional amendment that would achieve the result reached by the three-judge court in Texas. Without that amendment, however, he thought that the Constitution simply did not address the issue of school funding.

After the chief justice speaks, each justice presents his or her opinion to the conference. The justices speak in order of seniority: Justice William Douglas was next in line. Douglas, who had just celebrated his seventy-fourth birthday, was beginning his thirty-third year on the nation's highest court. One of the youngest individuals ever to join the Court when Franklin Roosevelt nominated him in 1939, Douglas had, throughout the years, become one of the Court's more controversial figures and one of its most consistently liberal voices. Now, Douglas was brief. Although he thought it naive to conclude that equalizing money would equalize educational opportunity, it was also wrong to conclude that money played no role. Therefore, explained Justice Douglas, he would vote to affirm the decision of the district court.

William Brennan, who spoke after Douglas, agreed with his senior colleague. After noting that "few cases have troubled me more," Justice Brennan explained that the real issue in this case was state action. Regardless of whether money was the crucial factor in education, the State of Texas, in deciding to play a role in financing education, was required to do so on an equal basis. Hinting that he agreed with Gochman's argument that the State of Texas should lose regardless of which legal test was applied, Brennan pointed out that, to his way of thinking, Texas had failed to demonstrate that its school financing plan was even related to any "rational interest." For this reason, Brennan explained, the district court decision was correct and ought to be affirmed.

Potter Stewart followed Brennan in order of seniority. Like Justice Brennan, Stewart had been nominated to the Court by President Eisenhower. Unlike Brennan, however, Justice Stewart could not be counted on to vote in any particular ideological direction. A pragmatist from Ohio, Justice Stewart was inclined to go his own way, and often found weaknesses in some of the traditional approaches taken by the Court. Picking up on the arguments of Justices Douglas and Brennan, Stewart was concerned about the role of money in education. He thought that the "budget of a school is a measure of quality of education" and provided "some index" that might be used to rank schools. Nevertheless, he was leaning toward reversing the three-judge court in Texas. The problem, said Stewart, was that the Equal Protection Clause of the Fourteenth Amendment did not apply to this type of situation. In order to find that a state action had violated the Equal Protection Clause, Stewart explained, one first had to show that a "discrete, specific, and identifiable class" had suffered discrimination. The adjectives "rich and poor," Stewart believed, do not denote such a distinct class. After hearing Stewart's presentation, Justice Powell concluded in his own notes that Stewart would vote to overturn the three-judge court in Texas. Douglas, however, was not so sure. In his notes, Douglas placed a question mark next to Stewart's name.

Justice Byron White, from Colorado, who spoke next, shared many qualities with his colleague from Ohio. A former Rhodes scholar who

{ *Chapter 7* }

had won the Heisman trophy and played professional football, White was not one to follow the crowd. Indeed, later that term White would break with a majority of the Court when he wrote a stinging dissent, joined only by Justice Rehnquist, in the controversial abortion case of *Roe v. Wade* (1973). In *Rodriguez*, he disagreed with both sides. There *was* an identifiable class in this case, said White, and it consisted of people who wanted more money for their schools but were "locked in" by the Texas financing system. White therefore concluded that the district court decision ought to be upheld. Nevertheless, White wanted a more narrow opinion than had been produced by the three-judge court. Rather than demanding absolute equality in funding, White thought that the Court should be clear in endorsing a system like district power equalizing that would not mandate equality but would free up districts that wanted to provide more for their students.

It was now Justice Thurgood Marshall's turn to address the conference. Although he had been ill during oral argument, perhaps no one, not even Justice Powell, was more familiar with this type of case. Marshall's mother had been a schoolteacher. Marshall had directed the NAACP Legal Defense and Education Fund And in that capacity had played an important role in organizing one of the most successful litigation strategies in history, culminating in the Supreme Court's decision in *Brown v. Board of Education*. Marshall thought that he had learned something in all those years, and he wanted to share it with his colleagues on the Court. He began by stating that education would never truly be equalized. Money, however, was different. The amount of dollars spent on school could, at least roughly, be made the same. The Texas school financing law, Marshall argued, resulted in what he called "geographic discrimination." This was his way of describing what Coons, Sugarman, and Clune had observed: The amount of money spent on a child's education was related to where that child resided. Geographic discrimination, concluded Marshall, did not "shape up with the Fourteenth Amendment." Consequently, the district court decision should be upheld.

Justice Harry Blackmun followed Marshall. Blackmun's name was soon to become almost a household word. Later that term, he would author the majority opinion in *Roe v. Wade*, one of the most controversial decisions ever handed down by the Court. His opinion in *Roe* was also symbolic, for it began Blackmun's break with his old friend,

Warren Burger. Both hailed from Minnesota, and when Blackmun first joined the Court, someone coined the phrase "Minnesota Twins" to refer to the pair. Over the next decade, Blackmun would stray from the more conservative chief justice.

In *Rodriguez*, however, Blackmun was in step with Burger. He expressed no doubt that the lower court decision should be reversed. As Blackmun saw it, the Texas system provided "an adequate, basic education." More to the point, however, Blackmun thought it "much safer to let states struggle with this." If courts were to mandate "equality in education," this would be, argued Blackmun, "another step towards big government." Moreover, Blackmun concluded, in an attempt to achieve equality, there might well be "a general lowering of educational standards."

Now it was time for the two newest justices on the Court to speak. Justices Powell and Rehnquist had been sworn in on the same day in early January, 1972. Powell's nomination was surrounded by very little controversy (save for some questions about his civil rights record), and he was actually confirmed by the Senate a week earlier than Rehnquist. Powell spoke before Rehnquist in conference.

Since Powell had already discussed the case with his clerks and sought out information from other sources, when it came time for him to speak to his brethren on this matter, he was well-prepared. The data on education funding in Virginia had arrived earlier in the day, and he integrated those numbers into a carefully organized set of notes that he brought with him to conference. There was no doubt in his mind that the three-judge district court's decision was, as he wrote in his notes, "regressive." He took issue with both the law and the facts as they were understood by the Texas court. The central question, he thought, was "whether education [was] a fundamental interest requiring application of the compelling interest test." Powell explained that although he had "no doubts about the importance of education — especially in a democracy," education was *not guaranteed* by the Constitution [emphasis in original]." In addition, he reminded his fellow justices that they had "never held that wealth [was] a badge of discrimination." Although it is not clear whether he said this at conference (no reference to it appears in Justice Douglas's notes), Powell, in his own notes, wrote that "to hold that wealth is suspect . . . is a communist doctrine but is not even accepted (except in a limited sense) in socialist countries."

Since there was no reason to invoke strict scrutiny, Powell argued that the State of Texas was only required to show that its funding system had a rational basis. He testified about his own experiences on the Richmond School Board, assuring the other members of the Court that local control of education was important. Also, since property tax–based financing was the norm in the United States, to overturn the Texas school financing system using this lower standard would be tantamount to saying that the "legislatures of the 49 states have been irrational for the last century." Then Powell began to refer to the report that had been forwarded to him from Virginia. Those numbers proved, argued Powell, that by remedying discrimination using a classification the Court had never before recognized, the Court risked harming members of minority groups who lived in urban areas. "Richmond," Powell explained, "has the largest black population and they get a larger tax return than most parts of VA. Richmond would drop from [spending] $800 to $600 [per student]. Arlington County spends $1300 per pupil — it too would drop. Those who would be hurt the most are those who can afford the hurt least." Powell concluded by admonishing his fellow justices that "only the legislative branch can fix and solve this problem."

Justice William Rehnquist was the last to speak. Rehnquist believed in an originalist approach to constitutional interpretation. For an originalist, interpretation begins at the time the portion of the Constitution in question "originated." It follows that originalist judges try to ascertain the meaning of sometimes murky constitutional language by studying the history that surrounds the adoption of the terms. Since *Rodriguez* involved the Fourteenth Amendment, Rehnquist thought it made sense to look back to 1868, when the amendment was ratified. This is what the Supreme Court had done in 1953 when it ordered that *Brown v. Board of Education* be reargued during the next term. "What evidence is there," the Court had asked then, "that the Congress which submitted, and the state legislatures and conventions which ratified the Fourteenth Amendment contemplated or did not contemplate, understood or did not understand, that it would abolish segregation in the public schools?"

When it came time to draft the majority opinion in *Brown*, Chief Justice Earl Warren determined the historical record to be inconclusive on this point. Rehnquist was clerking for Justice Jackson when

*Brown* was handed down. Now, as the newest justice on the Court, he rejected Warren's tentativeness. According to Douglas's notes, Rehnquist argued that "this kind of financing of school districts" was in place "at time of adoption of Fourteenth Amendment." Therefore, those who drafted the Equal Protection Clause would have been aware of the practice. The implication was that there was no evidence that the framers of the Fourteenth Amendment had any intention of changing how schools were funded. The new justice ended his comments by explaining that the accepted history of the Equal Protection Clause was that it was only intended to eliminate discrimination based on race. Absent any evidence that the State of Texas was engaging in "invidious gerrymandering" — that is, intentionally drawing school districts along racial lines — Rehnquist agreed with Justices Stewart and Powell that the proper test was rational basis. Rehnquist would vote to reverse the decision of the district court.

Counting up the votes, it appeared that it was five to four in favor of overturning the three-judge court in Texas. Since Chief Justice Burger was in the majority, it fell to him to make the opinion writing assignment. Since Powell clearly had the most interest in the case, at least among those in the majority, he was asked to draft the majority opinion.

# CHAPTER 8

# Chamber Deliberations

## Maintaining the Majority

Justice Louis Brandeis once commented that "the reason the public thinks so much of the Justices of the Supreme Court is that they are almost the only people in Washington who do their own work." Regardless of what the public thinks, or whether this was an accurate description of how the Supreme Court operated in the early twentieth century when Brandeis was on the bench, it was not that way by 1972, when Powell began working on his opinion in *Rodriguez*. As had become common practice, the first draft of the opinion was written by Powell's clerk, Larry Hammond. Ironically, Hammond was, at least initially, the only one of Powell's three clerks who agreed with the lower court's decision in *Rodriguez*. Nevertheless, by the time the opinion was released, Hammond had changed his mind. This, at least, was how Powell would remember the events a few years later in a letter that he sent to another clerk, J. Harvie Wilkinson, III.

Although Powell had Hammond write the actual draft of the opinion, the justice did not take a hands-off approach. He sent Hammond a continuous stream of memos indicating his views on the case. For example, on October 26, 1972, Powell wrote to Hammond that he had just read *Shapiro v. Thompson* (1969): "What attracted my attention is the brief concurring opinion by Justice Stewart." Powell suggested that Hammond incorporate a quote from Stewart's opinion into his draft opinion in *Rodriguez*.

Powell's reference to *Shapiro*, and particularly to Potter Stewart's concurring opinion, is telling. *Shapiro v. Thompson* represented cases from Alabama, Connecticut, and the District of Columbia that involved the constitutionality of waiting periods for full eligibility for certain public assistance programs. Justice Brennan wrote for the majority in *Shapiro*, finding that the waiting periods violated the constitutional right to interstate travel. According to Brennan's opinion, "the nature of our Federal Union and our constitutional concepts of personal liberty unite to require that all citizens be free to travel throughout the length and breadth of our land uninhibited by statutes, rules, or regulations which unreasonably burden or restrict this movement." In his dissent in *Shapiro*, Justice John Marshall Harlan claimed that what the majority had done was to "pick out particular human activities, characterize them as 'fundamental,' and give them added protection." Perhaps in response to Harlan, Stewart, who had written the opinion in the 1966 case *United States v. Guest*, which had first announced the right to interstate travel, felt compelled to draft a concurring opinion in *Shapiro* defending his earlier reasoning. Stewart insisted that the right to travel from state to state had not simply been selected at random by the Court. Rather, the Court in both *Guest* and *Shapiro*, had merely recognized "an established constitutional right."

The similarity between *Shapiro* and *Rodriguez* was that both cases involved the question of which rights the Court ought to recognize as fundamental. Many saw in the decisions of the Warren Court a willingness to expand the category of rights deemed fundamental. It was certainly possible to view *Guest* and *Shapiro* as having contributed to that theme, and to believe the plaintiffs in *Rodriguez* had asked the Court to take the next step and announce that the right to an education was fundamental. Powell clearly did not want to go in this direction. He was looking for a principled way of aligning the precedents so that they would not lead to this result. One of the benefits of Stewart's concurring opinion in *Shapiro* was that it pointed the way toward a more limiting formula: If in the past the Court had merely acknowledged rights already established, and if Powell could argue that the right to an education had not been previously established as a fundamental right under the Constitution, then Stewart's concurring opinion supported rejecting the claims of the plaintiffs in *Rodriguez*.

There may, however, have been another reason beyond potentially useful language in a similar case for Powell's interest in Stewart's then three-year-old opinion. Powell was writing for a slim five-member majority. Although it was not likely that any of the five justices who had voted with him at conference would switch sides and create a majority to uphold the lower court decision, it was possible that, in writing the opinion, Powell might lose the support of one of the justices for his majority reasoning. Although Powell might still have written "for the Court," an opinion onto which at least four other justices had not signed was known as a plurality opinion; its reasoning could not, by definition, claim the full authority of the Court.

Of those who were members of Powell's narrow majority, Stewart was the least predictable. Powell might have thought that, by quoting Stewart, he could be more confident the justice would sign onto his majority opinion. If this was Powell's intent, however, he was not, initially at least, successful. Powell's difficulties with Stewart would only grow in the weeks ahead.

On October 28, Larry Hammond sent two memos to Powell letting the justice know that the "meat of the opinion" would consist of a "discussion and interpretation of Supreme Court cases," and that he thought that the opinion should avoid extensive discussion of the data presented by both sides. Hammond informed Powell that the opinion would be organized around discussions of wealth as a suspect classification and whether there existed a fundamental constitutional interest in, or right to, an education. The terms right and interest are used interchangeably by the Court. In fact, Powell would later admit to Hammond that he was puzzled over "whether there is a difference between a 'fundamental right' and a 'fundamental interest.'" Powell suggested that it was easier to think of education as a fundamental interest than as a right.

Next to Hammond's mention of education as a fundamental interest, Powell added a note in the margin explaining that a "'fundamental interest' in a constitutional sense was one rooted in the Constitution itself." Powell planned to argue that if the Court were to "depart from this there are no benchmarks — only subjective judgments. E.g. Is education more 'fundamental' than feeding or housing, or protecting our citizens?" One sees in Powell's formula an attempt to build upon Stewart's earlier language in both *Guest* and *Shapiro*. Eventually, this approach would become central to Powell's opinion in *Rodriguez*. This argument, in fact, would later allow *Rodriguez* to become exactly what Powell had hoped it would be: a brake on the Warren Court's trend toward an expansive approach to equal protection.

By the middle of November, Hammond had completed a rough draft of the majority opinion in *Rodriguez*. Powell reviewed it approvingly, urging Hammond to continue to "give this case [his] first priority attention." The justice explained presciently that "the way this opinion is written could have profound influence on constitutional doctrine."

Early in December, Hammond delivered his first formal draft of the opinion to Powell. Powell had the draft sent to the print shop, but before making the printed draft available to all the justices, Powell first sent a copy to the one justice he was most worried about losing: Potter Stewart.

---

## A Problematic Precedent

On January 4, the draft opinion was circulated to the other chambers. Four days later, Justice Rehnquist indicated that he would join Powell's opinion. Then, on January 25, Powell penned a brief handwritten note to Larry Hammond. J. Harvie Wilkinson, III, another of Powell's clerks, had been discussing the case with both Hammond and Powell. Wilkinson had come across an article in the most recent issue of the *Harvard Law Review* he thought should be included in the *Rodriguez* opinion. The article had been authored by the noted Stanford law professor Gerald Gunther. Wilkinson thought that it would help to explain how *Rodriguez* was consistent with some of Powell's earlier opinions in equal protection cases. Powell recommended that Hammond follow Wilkinson's advice and include some quotes from the article in his draft of the majority opinion.

As it turns out, Wilkinson was not the only clerk who had been thinking about some of Powell's earlier work. These opinions had become a concern for Hammond. Although the justice had only been on the Court for part of the prior term, he had already begun to establish his approach to the Equal Protection Clause of the Fourteenth Amendment. Hammond was worried that Powell's previous approach might be more conducive to the dissenters than to Powell's majority opinion. Specifically, Hammond was concerned about the first opinion Powell had written for the Court in *Aetna v. Weber Casualty and*

*Surety Co.* (1972), the same case Gochman and Yudof had emphasized in their brief.

The two-tier approach to equal protection was not without its critics. As would soon become evident, Justice Stewart was one of those who took issue with at least part of the formulation. Justice Thurgood Marshall, however, also disliked the stark all-or-nothing protection for rights that often emerged from the standard. Dissenting in *Dandridge v. Williams* (1970), Marshall had rejected the two-tier approach, writing that when evaluating claims under the Equal Protection Clause "concentration must be placed upon the character of the classification in question, the relative importance to individuals in the class discriminated against of the governmental benefits that they do not receive, and the asserted state interests in support of the classification."

Had this "sliding scale approach" (as it was called) been adopted by the Court, it might have been beneficial to the plaintiffs in *Rodriguez*, since it was hard to disagree with the proposition that education, even if not identified as a fundamental constitutional interest, had a strong "relative importance" under the Constitution. Using the sliding scale approach, the state interest required in *Rodriguez* would have had to correspond with the amount of importance placed on education. There was some doubt about whether Texas would have been able to meet this increased burden. In fact, this was similar to the approach Hammond had recommended to Justice Powell earlier, before he knew that Powell would vote to overturn the district court.

Since Marshall had been the primary champion of this more flexible approach to equal protection, Hammond expected it to be at the core of the former civil rights leader's dissent. Therefore he saw Powell's opinion in *Weber* as a problem. As Hammond would explain many years later in a letter to Powell, "one line in the opinion . . . [was] suggestive of a version of the sliding scale approach to the Fourteenth Amendment."

Decided on April 24, 1972, *Weber* concerned the "right of dependent unacknowledged, illegitimate children to recover under Louisiana's workmen's compensation laws benefits for the death of their natural father." Powell's majority opinion found that the denial of such benefits to illegitimate children, when they were already awarded to legitimate children, was a violation of the Equal Protection Clause. He wrote: "The state interest in legitimate family relationships is not served by the statute; the state interest in minimizing problems of proof is not significantly disturbed by our decision. The inferior classification of dependent unacknowledged illegitimates bears, in this instance, no significant relationship to those recognized purposes of recovery which workmen's compensation statutes commendably serve." To Hammond, this bore a suspicious similarity to Marshall's dissent in *Dandridge*.

This concern brought Hammond back to the Gunther article. Entitled "In Search of Evolving Doctrine on a Changing Court: A Model for a Newer Equal Protection," the article reviewed the 1971 Supreme Court term. Gunther had singled out Powell for praise, and even mentioned the school funding cases and the work of Coons, Sugarman, and Clune as an example of how "to an unusual degree, litigation plans and doctrinal analysis came from the same hands." Gunther was most interested, however, in the evolution of the two-tiered approach to equal protection. He noted that "some strategists recognize that the open-endedness of fundamental interests might prove a fatal flaw: if the claims extended beyond schools and housing to golf courses and sewers, the sheer magnitude of the enterprise might stifle the Court's egalitarian zeal." In a section of the article subtitled "Thus Far and No Further," Gunther cited several cases including the majority opinions in *Dandridge* and *Jefferson v. Hackney* (1972) as evidence of the Burger Court's reluctance to continue the Warren Court's expansion of recognized fundamental interests. If this was all Gunther had written, Hammond probably would not have been reluctant to include references to the Gunther article in Powell's *Rodriguez* opinion. The Stanford law professor had gone on, however, to propose that there was "more to the Burger Court's reception of the strict scrutiny heritage than these stand pat ingredients of refusal to extend and retention of the best established." Here, he cited Powell's opinion in *Weber*, observing that it showed signs of an attempt to "blur the distinctions between strict and minimal scrutiny," an approach that Gunther argued had been consistently urged upon the Court by Justice Marshall. Since the last thing that Hammond wanted to do was draw attention to *Weber*, it made little sense to him to cite Gunther's article. Without specifically explaining this concern, Hammond tried to redirect Powell to other articles he thought might be more helpful. In the end, Hammond was successful: No mention of Gunther's article found its way into the majority opinion finally handed down by Powell.

_____

## Stewart's Memo

A second problem — also concerning the two-tiered standard — arrived on Powell's desk on February 8. On that day, a memo from Justice Stewart was delivered to Powell's chambers. Although addressed to Powell, the memo was circulated to all of the chambers. Stewart was responding to the *Rodriguez* draft opinion that had been circulated about a month earlier. The justice indicated that although he "agreed with the result" he was unable to "subscribe to an opinion that accepts the 'doctrine' that there are two separate alternative tests under the Equal Protection Clause, and that the necessary first step in any equal protection case is to decide which test to apply, and therefore first to decide whether a 'fundamental interest' is affected." Stewart wrote that he had "become convinced . . . that the theory that there is a 'compelling interest' [strict scrutiny] test and a quite different 'rational basis' test under the Equal Protection Clause is wholly spurious and unsound in the absence of a 'suspect' classification."

Although Stewart agreed that a law infringing upon an "individual liberty or freedom explicitly or implicitly guaranteed by the Constitution" was "presumptively invalid," this was not because the law failed a particular legal test but rather "because of the constitutional freedom" involved. In other words, Justice Stewart had adopted a somewhat absolutist position with regard to freedoms "explicitly or implicitly guaranteed by the Constitution." However, strict scrutiny, or as he was calling it, the "compelling state interest test," was only to be used in the event that the state had created a classification that, according to the Court's precedents, might be defined as "suspect."

From Stewart's perspective, Powell's draft opinion in *Rodriguez*, although not finding education to be a fundamental constitutional interest subject to strict scrutiny, nonetheless erred by tacitly accepting the notion that such an approach would be valid. The problem, explained Stewart, was that virtually all laws led to "treating some people differently from others." Since "there is hardly a statute on the books, therefore, that an ingenious lawyer cannot attack under the Equal Protection

Clause," should the lawyer be able to "persuade a court that a 'fundamental interest' is involved," Stewart worried that this approach could take the Court back to the "heyday of the Nine Old Men, who felt that the Constitution enabled them to invalidate almost any state laws they thought unwise." Given Powell's earlier note to Hammond about *Shapiro*, it is interesting that in a postscript to this memo Stewart advises that he had done a better job of expressing all of this in his "concurring opinion in the *Shapiro* case [citation omitted]."

Stewart's memo drew immediate attention from both Hammond and Powell. It did not help matters that Justice Rehnquist, who only a month earlier had signed onto Powell's draft, now indicated that he shared some of Stewart's concerns. Indeed, Rehnquist advised Powell that he was now considering joining both the opinions of Powell and Stewart. On February 12, Justice Blackmun sent a note to Powell in which he expressed agreement with Rehnquist. Blackmun warned that if Powell and Stewart were not able to resolve their differences, he might feel obliged to follow Rehnquist and join both opinions. This was serious. There was now a very real threat that Powell's opinion would not only fail to garner the support of at least four other justices but would barely speak for a plurality of the Court. At Powell's urging, Blackmun agreed to not share his threat with the rest of the Court. Instead, Blackmun issued a memo joining Powell's opinion and expressed interest "in the suggestions that Potter has advanced."

―――――――

## Resolution

As Powell shared with Blackmun, he thought he had no choice but to use the two-tier model. He felt strongly about *stare decisis*, the principle that judges ought to abide by prior cases. To Powell, it was this willingness to follow the decisions of other judges that both differentiated and legitimated courts in the eyes of the American people. The justice's reading of available equal protection precedents led him to what he thought was an inescapable conclusion: the two-tier approach was now settled law.

Powell wanted evidence to use to convince his fellow justices that this was indeed the case, and he asked Hammond to compile a list of all of the major cases in which the Court had identified a fundamental right and applied strict scrutiny. Hammond responded with a memo containing the names of thirteen cases, and identifying a potential pitfall for Powell. He wrote, "Although every Justice has at least joined in opinions using the two-tiered approach, your closest allies are on the other side." In parentheses, Hammond summed up the difficulty with a humorous analogy: "There's nothing wrong with the dog food [. . .] we're just selling it to the wrong dogs."

After holding a meeting with his clerks to go over the situation with Justice Stewart, Powell was finally ready to respond on February 14. He began his memo by assuring Stewart that "little of substance" separated them. Then, he carefully laid out his understanding of Stewart's objections. Of particular importance both to the negotiations between the two justices and to Powell's final opinion for the Court was the discussion of fundamental rights. "I am in entire agreement," Powell wrote, "that a 'fundamental' rights test which allows judges to pick and choose rights which they desire to accord special protection . . . would be unacceptable." This was not, however, how Powell thought that test had been used. As he had written in his draft opinion in *Rodriguez*, Powell explained, a fundamental right had to either have "roots in the Constitution" or "must be fundamental 'in a constitutional sense.' " Rights that were not "explicitly or implicitly guaranteed by the Constitution" were not included in this formulation. After once again reminding Stewart that "we are not far apart," Powell concluded his memo by opening the door to "any changes [that Stewart] might suggest."

Stewart, Blackmun, and Rehnquist were not the only justices with concerns. While this dispute was going on, Chief Justice Burger added his own commentary. When discussing whether or not education was a fundamental right, Powell's opinion had at one point made reference to "the present context," suggesting that the facts in *Rodriguez* made it a poor vehicle for the establishment of a right. Burger was afraid that any reference to "the present context" was unnecessary and might simply invite litigants to present a better fact challenge to the Court. In an unusually harsh response, Powell dismissed the chief justice's observation, arguing that "any decent attorney will tell his clients that, after all the ways in which we foreclose the result, the ball game is over."

On the same day Powell sent his memo to Justice Stewart, he received the first draft of Justice Marshall's dissenting opinion. Marshall had played into Powell's worst fears. After reviewing the dissent, Powell wrote in the corner of his copy that "The rationale of this opinion — that each school district must have the same 'property wealth' would apply to all local subdivisions and in the end perhaps to the states." Next to where Marshall referred to the "variations in the degree of care with which this Court will scrutinize particular classifications" Powell wrote in the margin "WOW!" He repeated this comment on the back of Marshall's draft after summarizing Marshall's call for equal funding. Powell wondered, in a note to Hammond, why Marshall had not addressed the negative effect equal funding might have on urban districts. Of all of Marshall's claims, Powell seemed most offended by the charge that local control over the schools is "an excuse only." This argument was seen by Powell as an attack on an institution upon which he placed great value. Next to this line in Marshall's dissent, Powell wrote "not so." He also penned a note to Hammond about this, declaring based on his own "personal experience" that "local school boards in Virginia have far more operational responsibility than the State Board of Education."

But Marshall's dissent was not Powell's biggest concern. The key to maintaining majority support for his opinion was still Potter Stewart. On Powell's instructions, Hammond made some changes to the draft opinion in hopes of bringing Stewart on board. Specifically, in the section of the opinion that introduced the plaintiffs' claim that a fundamental right was violated, Hammond added the following subtle language: "It is this question — whether education is a fundamental right, *in the sense that it is among the rights and liberties protected by the Constitution* — which has so consumed the attention of courts and commentators in recent years" [emphasis added]. Hammond had managed to discretely redefine the education funding cases, so that the focus was now upon whether the right to an education was "among the rights and liberties protected by the Constitution."

Powell was clearly pleased with Hammond's new draft, complimenting him on "an excellent job." This new version of the opinion was circulated on February 23, and it immediately had the desired effect: Three days later, Justice Stewart, specifically citing the changes that Hammond had made, agreed to join Powell's opinion. Although Stewart thought he might still file a separate concurring opinion, his agreement to join Powell virtually guaranteed that the justice would now write for a true majority. Blackmun officially joined Powell's opinion on that same day, followed about two weeks later by the chief justice. On March 13, Powell circulated his final draft. He had held onto his majority and in the process drafted an opinion that would have a tremendous impact on U.S. law and society. All that remained was to announce it to the public.

# CHAPTER 9

# The Decision

## Powell versus Marshall

By tradition, the Supreme Court hands down most of its decisions in open court. Oftentimes, the justices read portions of the opinion from the bench. So it was on the morning of March 21, 1973. Justice Powell had prepared a summary of the case that ran approximately four pages. By the time he read the third paragraph, it was clear that Gochman had lost: "We disagree with the District Court," Powell said, "and reverse its judgment."

When Powell returned to his chambers there was a handwritten note waiting for him. It was from Larry Hammond. The young clerk told the justice how much he had enjoyed working on *Rodriguez*. Although he was not fully convinced of the fairness of the school funding systems in place in Texas, Hammond thought that Powell's opinion was consistent with constitutional doctrine.

Powell replied that afternoon. He thanked Hammond for his "generous sentiments," and tried to reassure the clerk about the decision in *Rodriguez*. "I believe," wrote Powell, "that our decision may well lead to needed improvements in a more orderly way."

Powell's colleague on the Court, Thurgood Marshall, saw things differently. Dissenting in *Rodriguez*, Marshall aimed his pen at Powell's optimism: "The Court's suggestion of legislative redress and experimentation will doubtless be of great comfort to the school-children of Texas' disadvantaged districts, but considering the vested interests of wealthy school districts in the preservation of the status quo, they are worth little more."

Given its author, the argumentative tone of the dissent should come as no surprise. If one were to write a fictional legal novel about equality and the public schools, one could not develop a better antagonist for Powell than Marshall, nor a better case in which their rivalry was likely to surface than *Rodriguez*.

Justice Lewis Powell was the quintessential southern gentleman. Raised in an aristocratic family in Richmond, Powell had attended Washington and Lee University in Lexington, Virginia. Lexington was in the heart of the old Confederacy, and the college was named after the Confederate leader, General Robert E. Lee, who is buried on the university's grounds. Prior to Lewis Powell, the most famous graduate of Washington and Lee Law School was John W. Davis. Davis had almost preceded Powell on the Supreme Court. He had rejected a possible appointment and instead ran unsuccessfully as the Democratic Party's nominee for president in 1924.

Late in his career, Davis would pit his skills against Thurgood Marshall, arguing for South Carolina in one of the cases that collectively made up *Brown v. Board of Education*. When Lewis Powell was first graduated from law school, a job offer came from Davis's New York law firm. Powell turned it down, deciding instead to return to Richmond and take a job with one of that city's most prestigious firms: Hunton, Williams, Anderson, Gray, and Moore. Interestingly, this was the firm retained by Prince Edward County when defending itself in *Brown*'s Virginia component, *Davis v. School Board of Prince Edward County* (1954).

In *Rodriguez*, it is likely that Marshall envisioned himself continuing the fight he had begun almost twenty years earlier when he stepped before the Court to argue *Brown*. Once again, his opponent was a white southerner. Indeed, from Marshall's perspective, *Rodriguez* followed logically from *Brown*, and Powell's ties to that earlier case, if Marshall was aware of all of them, must have seemed bitterly ironic.

Initially, most commentators were sympathetic to Marshall, and Powell's majority opinion in *Rodriguez* was the subject of negative commentary almost from the moment of its release. Even one of Powell's clerks, J. Harvie Wilkinson, III, got involved. Wilkinson wrote an article in the *Virginia Law Review* that, although not necessarily critical of the result reached in *Rodriguez*, took issue with Powell's approach to equal protection analysis. Wilkinson was followed by prominent law professors such as Laurence Tribe, Erwin Chemerinsky, Ronald Dworkin, and Cass Sunstein. All of these writers agreed that Powell's opinion amounted to a crabbed reading of the Fourteenth Amendment. Indeed, it remains difficult to find articles that give unqualified support to the majority opinion in *Rodriguez*.

Absent from most of these articles, and perhaps even from Marshall's dissent, however, is an honest understanding of why Powell adopted the reasoning that he did in *Rodriguez* (Wilkinson's article was, of course, an exception). As Powell addressed the case, he was guided by two complementary goals. The first of these might be termed "political/factual," and the other was institutional.

*Rodriguez* stands out among Powell's opinions because of the justice's intimate knowledge of the subject matter. Even three years after the decision was handed down, in a letter Powell wrote to Wilkinson responding to his former clerk's article, the justice continued to articulate his concern that if the states took over funding the public schools, "state control [would become] inevitable." He emphasized, as he almost always did when writing about *Rodriguez*, that he "[knew] this from personal experience." Also, Powell still saw no reason why, if *Rodriguez* had been decided differently, the Fifth Amendment would not "require that the federal government equalize education and other public services among the 50 states." This sort of centralized control was anathema to Powell.

There was, however, an additional factor at work in Powell's opinion in *Rodriguez*. Powell firmly believed that it was not the role of the Court, as an institution, to right all of society's wrongs. Powell never made this more clear than in a speech he gave in 1982, almost a decade after delivering his opinion in *Rodriguez*. The subject of the speech was Footnote 4 of *United States v. Carolene Products* (1938), and Powell's main point was that the intent of Justice Stone, the author of the famous footnote, had been exaggerated through the years. "The problem," as Powell described it, was that, "in a democratic society there are inevitably winners and losers." For a judge to conclude from the simple fact that a group was disadvantaged by the results of the legislative process that the process violated the Equal Protection Clause required that the judge "have a substantive vision of what results the process should have yielded." Among the cases that he used to illustrate this argument was *Rodriguez*.

Implicit in Powell's speech was a criticism of the Warren Court. Indeed, in discussing *Rodriguez* in his speech, Powell brought up *Brown v. Board of Education* as a possible precedent for a different outcome. Although the Court was surely right to order desegregation, said Powell, "there are — there have to be — stopping points." *Rodriguez* was that stopping point. Indeed, as Wilkinson would later put it, *Rodriguez* represented "the foremost decision of judicial forbearance." And that was as Powell intended it.

## The Majority Opinion

Powell's opinion in *Rodriguez* began with a review of the basic facts of the case, including a brief history of school funding in Texas as well as a comparison between the Edgewood and Alamo Heights school districts. Powell concluded this section, which consumes almost one-quarter of his fifty-four page opinion, with an admission that despite the improvements that had been made in the school funding program in Texas, "substantial interdistrict disparities in school expenditures . . . in San Antonio and in varying degrees throughout the State still exist." In addition, Powell noted that "Texas virtually concedes that its . . . system of financing education could not withstand . . . strict judicial scrutiny." Therefore, the question that the Court had to answer was "whether the Texas system of financing public education operates to the disadvantage of some suspect class or impinges upon a fundamental right explicitly or implicitly protected by the Constitution, thereby requiring strict judicial scrutiny."

Powell moved to his analysis of the suspect classification claim by raising two questions. The first involved how the Court was to determine with any precision the class that had fallen victim to the alleged discrimination. Powell decided that there were actually three methods that one might use to define the wealth classification urged by Arthur Gochman and the appellees. It might be argued, for example, that "the poor" were all those who fell below a predetermined income level. Or, a relative measure might be used, defining the wealth class according to how much richer or poorer one set of individuals was when compared to another set. Finally, the class might be determined by measuring district wealth, relying only on the total wealth per pupil within a school district.

Powell argued that only the first measure — an absolute measure of individual poverty — fit with the wealth classifications used in prior cases. There were, however, problems with the application of these precedents to the situation in *Rodriguez*. Powell had identified one difficulty fairly early in his deliberations, spurred perhaps by Larry Hammond's recollections about his own situation growing up in Texas and attending a school that did not reflect his family's economic condition. *Districts* do not have rights, and the correlation between district wealth and individual wealth had not, according to Powell, been conclusively established. Indeed, Powell cited the *Yale Law Journal* article used by Wright during oral argument to point out that, at least in Connecticut, no correlation had been found.

But even if a direct relationship could be found between district and individual (or family) wealth, Powell maintained, the precedents relied upon by Gochman and the plaintiffs were not necessarily applicable. In cases such as *Bullock v. Carter* (1972), in which filing fees for election ballot access were found to violate the Fourteenth Amendment, an absolute deprivation of a right had been demonstrated. Those who lacked funds were not able to have their names appear on a ballot. In *Rodriguez*, however, poor students were still able to receive an education. Perhaps it was not the same education afforded wealthier children, or children who lived in wealthier districts; nevertheless, wrote Powell, "the Equal Protection Clause does not require absolute equality or precisely equal advantages."

This observation brought Powell to the next claim raised by the plaintiffs. Using the phrasing adopted to secure Justice Stewart's vote, Powell explained that *Rodriguez* also involved a dispute over "whether education is a fundamental right, in the sense that it is among the rights and liberties protected by the Constitution." Powell began his investigation of this question by approvingly quoting Chief Justice Warren's observation in *Brown* about "the importance of education to our democratic society." No one could seriously doubt Powell's belief in the civic importance of education; however, his support for civic education was always linked to his fear of Soviet-style communism. This concern was evidenced in the speeches he had made after returning from a visit to the Soviet Union in 1955, and even in the notes that he made for himself as he deliberated about *Rodriguez*. So, although asserting that "nothing this Court holds today in any way detracts from our historic dedication to public education," Powell was not prepared to render a decision that might lead to the very centralization of authority he associated with communism. Even the way Powell chose to explain education's role in society demonstrates this concern. The three-judge district court had ruled in favor of the plaintiffs based in part on "the grave significance of education to both the individual and to society." In addressing this claim in his opinion, Powell subtly changed the direction of the relationship. Whereas the three-judge panel had insisted upon education's "significance . . . to society," Powell's opinion speaks of education as an activity "performed by the State" presumably for the benefit of the individuals, not of society.

Notwithstanding this focus on the individual, if the Court determined education to be a fundamental right, the result, after applying strict scrutiny — or so Powell had concluded — would be the transfer of control over education from the local school board to the state government, or perhaps even to the federal government. In the process of mandating this shift, of course, the Court would also be expanding its own unchecked, counterdemocratic power. Powell would have none of this. Along with the need to secure the fifth vote in *Rodriguez*, Powell's antipathy for centralization helps explain why he cited Stewart's concurring opinion in *Shapiro*. For it is when he began analyzing the "right to an education" that Powell inserted Stewart's language. Powell concluded that the "lesson" of cases such as *Dandridge v. Williams* (1970) and *Jefferson v. Hackney* (1972) "[was] plain. It is not the province of this Court to create substantive constitutional rights in the name of guaranteeing equal protection of the laws." In order to discover whether the right to an education is fundamental, Powell explained, one need only "[assess] whether there is a right to an education explicitly or implicitly guaranteed by the Constitution." Dismissing Gochman's claim both at oral argument and in his brief that there was a nexus between the right to an education and the constitutional rights to speak and vote, Powell stated that "the Court has never presumed to possess either the ability or the authority to guarantee to the citizenry the most effective speech or the most informed electoral choice."

Powell's finding that the right to an education was neither "explicitly or implicitly" protected by the Constitution, coupled with his earlier determination that Texas had not created a suspect classification, meant that the proper test to be applied to *Rodriguez* was the rational basis standard. If the State of Texas could demonstrate that its financing system was rationally related to a legitimate state interest, then the lower court decision would have to be overturned.

Here again, Powell's background on the Richmond School Board played into his analysis. He had concluded from his own experience that local control over the schools was real and not a "mere sham," as Justice Marshall had asserted in his dissenting opinion. In an attached footnote to *Rodriguez*, Powell detailed the many functions performed by the local school boards in Texas. Although Texas's school financing plan was, Powell admitted, far from perfect, it represented an attempt to balance the state's desire to provide adequate funds for education with its important interest in maintaining this local control over the schools. The argument that other, more equitable systems might still balance these two factors was not persuasive, thought Powell, because under the rational basis standard the means chosen to advance the state's legitimate interests need only be rationally related to those ends. "In sum," Powell wrote, "to the extent that the Texas system of school financing results in unequal expenditures between children who happen to reside in different districts, we cannot say that such disparities are the product of a system that is so irrational as to be invidiously discriminatory."

Powell ended his opinion with what he called a "cautionary postscript" about the "unprecedented upheaval in public education" that would result from decisions such as those made by the California Supreme Court in *Serrano v. Priest* (1971) and the district court in *Rodriguez*. It was not that Powell was afraid of upsetting the status quo. His concern, he explained, was based on some evidence that the proposed revisions might have unintended negative consequences. Here, Powell returned to data that had bothered him from the start: "Several research projects," he wrote, "concluded that any financing alternative designed to achieve a greater equality of expenditures is likely to lead to higher taxation and lower educational expenditures in major urban areas." The footnote, ironically, pointed toward the study conducted by Berke.

This concern led to the final paragraph of Powell's opinion, which deserves to be quoted in full since it rather succinctly summarizes all that the justice was trying to communicate:

> These practical considerations, of course, play no role in the adjudication of the constitutional issues presented here. But they serve to

highlight the wisdom of the traditional limitations on the Court's function. The consideration and initiation of fundamental reforms with respect to state taxation and education are matters reserved for the legislative processes of the various States, and we do no violence to values of federalism and separation of powers by staying our hand. We hardly need add that this Court's action today is not to be viewed as placing its judicial imprimatur on the status quo. The need is apparent for reform in tax systems which may well have relied too long and too heavily on the local property tax. And certainly innovative thinking as to public education, its methods, and its funding is necessary to assure both a higher level of quality and greater uniformity of opportunity. These matters merit the continued attention of the scholars who already have contributed much by their challenges. But the ultimate solutions must come from the lawmakers and from the democratic pressures of those who elect them.

## Justice Stewart's Concurring Opinion

Justice Potter Stewart, as he had indicated that he might, filed a separate concurring opinion. This opinion followed closely the reasoning and even the wording of his February 8, 1972, memo to Powell. In the end, however, Stewart did not abandon Powell's opinion, but instead insisted that *Rodriguez* had applied, and thus reinforced, Stewart's basic understanding of equal protection analysis, with its rejection of the two-tier approach. In truth, and despite Stewart's attempt to recast what Powell had done, however, the majority opinion in *Rodriguez* did not signal the death knell for the two-tier approach to the Equal Protection Clause. Instead, it helped to etch that approach deeper into the fabric of the Court's jurisprudence. Indeed, perhaps no one understood this better — nor was more upset by that fact — than Justice Thurgood Marshall.

## Justice Marshall's Dissent

After Chief Justice Burger had assigned the majority opinion to Justice Powell, the dissenters in the case — Justices White, Douglas,

Brennan, and Marshall — organized their response. Eventually, all but Douglas would draft dissents. Nevertheless, the most prominent, and by far the longest dissent came from an expected source: Thurgood Marshall. This was the plan from the start. On October 25, 1972, Justice Brennan sent a memo to Justice Douglas in which he asked for the senior justice's approval on an agreement that "Thurgood will do *Rodriguez* and I will do *Columbia Broadcasting* [*v. Democratic National Committee* (1973)]. Douglas indicated that this was "fine with him."

As it turned out, Brennan still wrote a brief dissent, in which he argued that the right to an education was fundamental since it was "inextricably linked to the right to participate in the electoral process and to the rights of free speech and association guaranteed by the First Amendment." Justice White also dissented. In an opinion that ran a bit longer than Brennan's, White insisted on the kind of "invigorated rationality scrutiny" that Gerald Gunther had advocated in his 1972 *Harvard Law Review* article. "It [was] not enough," argued White, "that the Texas system . . . [sought] to achieve the valid, rational purpose of maximizing local initiative; the means chosen . . . must also be rationally related to the end sought to be achieved." White thought that the "local initiative" intended by the Texas system was thwarted in school districts that lacked the property wealth to act on those initiatives.

White's dissent, given the trend that had been identified by Gunther, might have become more significant had it been adopted in future cases. The Court has, at times, used a more rigorous third or "middle tier" level of scrutiny in affirmative action and gender discrimination cases. For example, in *Craig v. Boren*, a case handed down in December of 1976, the Court, with Powell's guarded approval, used a legal test that seemed to fall somewhere between the two tiers of review generally applied. The case involved an allegation of gender-based discrimination, and Powell, in a concurring opinion, noted that "candor compels the recognition that the relatively deferential 'rational basis' standard of review normally applied takes on a sharper focus when we address a gender-based classification." Interestingly, he cited Gunther's article, along with a piece somewhat critical of *Rodriguez* drafted by his former clerk, J. Harvie Wilkinson, III, in support of this position. Still, the Court has not departed much from its pre-*Rodriguez* approach to the Equal Protection Clause. The major candidate to displace the rigid two-tier standard, at least throughout most of the years following *Rodriguez*, was not the invigorated rational basis standard advocated by White, but its close cousin, the "sliding scale" method that Marshall had championed in *Dandridge*.

Marshall's dissent in *Rodriguez*, however, is remembered for more than just its insistence on a different test for analyzing equal protection claims. The dissent was in fact much more sweeping in its criticism, attacking point by point Powell's argument in favor of the Texas school financing system.

Marshall opened his dissent by arguing that "the majority's holding can only be seen as a retreat from our historic commitment to equality in educational opportunity and as an unsupportable acquiescence in a system which deprives children in their earliest years of the chance to reach their full potential as citizens." Quoting from *Brown*, he reminded his fellow justices that the Court had warned of the damage that a poor education can have on children, "[affecting] their hearts and minds in a way unlikely ever to be undone."

Marshall reviewed what he saw as the important facts in the case, emphasizing the disparities identified by Berke in his affidavit and pointing out that Texas had not denied that these gaps between rich and poor districts existed. Again, Marshall returned to the earlier desegregation cases, including those that had served as precedents for *Brown*. He argued that in those cases the Court "acknowledged that inequality in the educational facilities provided to students may be discriminatory state action as contemplated by the Equal Protection Clause." If there was no link between school district wealth and the quality of education provided, then why, Marshall wanted to know, had "a number of our country's wealthiest school districts" demonstrated such a strong interest in the outcome of *Rodriguez*?

In response to both Powell's and Stewart's claims that there was no identifiable class of individuals who were being discriminated against in Texas, Marshall offered that "the overarching form of discrimination in this case is between the schoolchildren of Texas on the basis of the taxable property wealth of the districts in which they happen to live." The only real question, he argued, was whether this particular form of discrimination violated the Fourteenth Amendment.

Given the issues involved, however, the use of the rational basis standard in the case was, in Marshall's words, "an emasculation of the Equal Protection Clause."

It was at this point in his dissent that Marshall repeated his call, first articulated in *Dandridge*, for a more flexible equal protection standard. "The task in every case," Marshall wrote, "should be to determine the extent to which constitutionally guaranteed rights are dependent on interests not mentioned in the Constitution. As the nexus between the specific constitutional guarantee and the nonconstitutional interest draws closer, the nonconstitutional interest becomes more fundamental and the degree of judicial scrutiny applied when the interest is infringed on a discriminatory basis must be adjusted accordingly." He insisted that this was the approach the Court had in fact used over the years.

In addition to examining the relative significance of the right denied by disparate treatment when calibrating the degree of scrutiny given to a classification, Marshall insisted, the Court also considered what he referred to as the "invidiousness" of the discrimination involved. The term "invidious," as used by the Court, is difficult to define. Basically, an invidious classification is one the Court finds particularly harmful or offensive. Marshall provided several cases in which "the particularly invidious character of the classification caused the Court to pause and scrutinize with more than traditional care the rationality of state discrimination." His final example in this line of cases must have made Larry Hammond glad that he had dissuaded Powell from citing Gunther's *Harvard Law Review* article for fear of drawing attention to *Weber*. For, as Marshall then explained, "the Court's sensitivity to the invidiousness of the basis for discrimination . . . was most apparent" in *Weber*.

When defending the connection between education and other "basic constitutional values," Marshall's writing — as might have been expected — most reflected his history as a civil rights leader. Marshall pointed out that the states clearly understood the importance of education, since nearly every state constitution contained language mandating the provision of public education. Quoting case after case, Marshall explained why this was so by tying education to basic First Amendment guarantees as well as to political participation. The justice even cited data from earlier presidential elections that showed how education led to increased voter turnout. All of this, thought Marshall, "[compelled the Court] to recognize the fundamentality of education and to scrutinize with appropriate care the bases for state discrimination affecting equality of educational opportunity in Texas."

As Marshall had explained earlier, however, he was not only concerned about the importance of education, but about the nature of the discrimination alleged by the appellees. Citing Warren Court precedents, Marshall insisted that the "Court [had] frequently recognized that discrimination on the basis of wealth may create a classification of a suspect character and thereby call for exacting judicial scrutiny." Marshall claimed that even more importantly, unlike personal wealth, the group or district wealth that formed the basis for the disparate treatment in *Rodriguez* was beyond the control of the victims (the children). The implication was clear: In this case, wealth was as immutable as race; also, the poverty into which children were born — through no fault of their own — closely resembled the hardships and stigma faced by illegitimate children recognized in Powell's opinion in *Aetna v. Weber Casualty and Surety Company* (1972). Furthermore, Marshall wrote, "it is the State that has created the local school districts, and tied educational funding to the local property tax and thereby to local district wealth."

Marshall thought these precedents led to the inescapable conclusion that something more than the rational basis standard ought to apply in *Rodriguez*. Nevertheless, he cited approvingly the three-judge district court in Texas, which had determined that the State of Texas had "[failed] even to establish a reasonable basis for these classifications." Of Marshall's entire dissenting opinion, it was this section that most offended Justice Powell. For Marshall wrote that "local control is offered primarily as an excuse, rather than as a justification for interdistrict inequality." Just as Marshall felt affection and passion for the civil rights cases to which he had dedicated much of his adult life, Powell was enamored with the local school board. When Powell first received a copy of the draft dissent, he wrote "not so" next to Marshall's dismissal of local control as an "excuse." As already mentioned, in a footnote to his majority opinion explicitly addressed to "Mr. Justice Marshall," Powell detailed the many functions specifically assigned to the local school board by the Texas legislature. Still, Marshall insisted that all this was irrelevant since, regardless of what a local school board may have wanted to do, "the quality of the educational opportunity offered by any particular district is largely determined by the amount of taxable property located in the district — a factor over which local voters can exercise no control." It was also misleading, thought Marshall, to insist that by upholding the lower court's decision, the Supreme Court would somehow be mandating centralized control over the schools. In a long footnote, Marshall mentioned at least three other possible approaches to remedying the constitutional defeat. Chief among them was "the much discussed theory of district power equalization put forth by Professors Coons, Clune, and Sugarman."

Marshall's sarcastic comment at the end of his *Rodriguez* dissent that "the Court's suggestion of legislative redress and experimentation will doubtless be of great comfort to the schoolchildren of Texas' disadvantaged districts" — was aimed at Justice Powell's insistence that "the ultimate solutions [to school funding problems] must come from the lawmakers and from the democratic pressures of those who elect them." In retrospect, the results are mixed. The "innovative thinking" Justice Powell hoped for did occur. It was not, however, primarily driven by the "democratic pressures" referenced in his opinion. Although it is true that some state legislatures, on their own, made considerable and successful reforms to their school funding programs, in many other states, the pressure came from court challenges based on state constitutional guarantees. Indeed, the school funding cases that followed in the wake of *Rodriguez* are perhaps the best example of what has become known as "judicial federalism."

# CHAPTER 10

# Aftermath

## Judicial Federalism, Texas and Beyond

### Adequate and Independent State Grounds

Four years after the *Rodriguez* decision, Justice Brennan, who had dissented in that case, published an influential article in the *Harvard Law Review* entitled "State Constitutions and the Protection of Individual Rights." Brennan was troubled by what he saw as a conservative tilt on the Court that began when Warren Burger replaced Earl Warren as chief justice and continued with the addition of Rehnquist and Powell to the Court in 1972. The result, according to Brennan, was a Court that was not giving a sufficiently broad interpretation to the rights and liberties protected by the Constitution. He suggested that a remedy might be found in the actions of state court judges, who were already using state constitutions to grant more protection for rights than would otherwise be required by the federal Constitution. This principle of "judicial federalism" would soon receive support from an unlikely ally: William Rehnquist.

A few years earlier, in 1968, Justice Thurgood Marshall had written an opinion for the Court in which he found that free speech protections offered by the First and Fourteenth Amendments extended into privately owned shopping plazas. In that case, *Food Employees v. Logan Valley Plaza*, a labor union had been prevented from picketing in a parking area in front of a grocery store. The grocery store was located within a private shopping plaza, and the plaza's owner felt that he had the right to control the activities that went on in his parking lot. The Court disagreed, concluding that such lots are the "functional equivalents" of public streets and sidewalks. Therefore, those who had picketed had exercised protected First Amendment free expression rights.

By 1976 (perhaps not coincidentally the same year that Justice Brennan's article on judicial federalism appeared), in *Hudgens v. National Labor Relations Board (NLRB),* the Court changed its mind and overturned *Logan Valley.* Justice Stewart's majority opinion concluded that privately owned malls, sidewalks, and parking lots could not be equated with publicly owned property, and were therefore outside the reach of the First and Fourteenth Amendments.

*Hudgens* was the precedent that applied a few years later when several high school students set up a card table in the center courtyard of the Prune Yard shopping plaza in Campbell, California. The students wanted to pass out literature and seek signatures opposing a UN resolution. After a security guard ordered them to leave, they filed suit against the owners of the plaza in California state court. Eventually, the California Supreme Court ruled in favor of the students, concluding that their actions were protected not by the First and Fourteenth Amendments of the U.S. Constitution but rather by the free speech and expression articles in the California Constitution. The case was appealed to the U.S. Supreme Court, which affirmed the California court's decision in an opinion authored by William Rehnquist and joined by Brennan. In his opinion, Rehnquist, one of the conservative appointments to the Court that had triggered Brennan's article, championed the argument Brennan had made in his *Harvard Law Review* article. Rehnquist wrote that states retained the right to establish individual liberties "more expansive than those conferred by the Federal Constitution."

Judicial federalism, as this has come to be called, was not a new idea. Since at least 1874, the Supreme Court had recognized, in some form, what had come to be known as the "adequate and independent state grounds" doctrine. Basically, this doctrine limited the ability of the Supreme Court to review decisions of state courts. The reasoning was that, if state law was "adequate" to decide a case, and if a decision on a case could be made on grounds that were "independent" of any federal law or constitutional provision, then the Supreme Court, as an instrument of the federal government, had no power to evaluate or review the decision.

One must be careful not to exaggerate the scope of this doctrine. A state may not, for example, immunize a decision granting less protection to individual rights than might be offered by accepted interpretations of the federal Constitution. More importantly, state courts must assert, in no uncertain terms, that their decision rests squarely upon their state's constitution. This is not difficult, however, since state constitutions often contain provisions paralleling those contained in the federal Bill of Rights. For example, Article I, section 3 of the Ohio Constitution comes very close to the First Amendment, stating that "The people have the right to assemble together, in a peaceable manner, to consult for their common good; to instruct their representatives; and to petition the general assembly for the redress of grievances." Article I, section 3a of the Texas Constitution offers its own version of the Equal Protection Clause of the Fourteenth Amendment, declaring that "Equality under the law shall not be denied or abridged because of sex, race, color, creed, or national origin."

By cutting off the possibility of federal relief in the area of school finance cases, *Rodriguez* helped to fuel the expansion of judicial federalism. Indeed, in the years since *Rodriguez* was decided, at least thirty-two states have become embroiled in school funding litigation because of *Rodriguez;* all of these cases have been grounded in state constitutional guarantees. In half of these states, those who sought to overturn state funding regimes were successful. The courts that have heard these cases, however, cognizant of the "lack of judicially manageable standards" that have always plagued school funding cases, have generally stopped at simply declaring constitutional violations. The issue then returned to the state legislatures, which were expected to design new funding systems that might be looked on more favorably by the courts. The result has been round after round of court challenges that in some cases have lasted for decades. This is in fact what has happened in Texas following the *Rodriguez* decision, where one judge wondered whether he and his colleagues had been "assigned to some judicial purgatory where we must hear the same case over and over."

## Texas

Defeat in the Supreme Court ended neither the debate nor the litigation over school funding in Texas. Justice Powell's opinion could hardly be read as a ringing note of approval for the status quo, and the Texas legislature, in both 1975 and 1979, made some changes to the state's funding scheme, including altering the formula used to calculate the required state funds and establishing an additional level of state funding for poor districts. These latter monies were called State Equalization Aid. Still, significant disparities between rich and poor districts remained. Indeed, as Justice Alberto Gonzalez of the Supreme Court of Texas (who would later serve as the U.S. attorney general under President George W. Bush) described the situation: "In some areas of the state, education resembled a motorcycle with a 1,000-gallon fuel tank, and in other areas it resembled a tractor-trailer being fueled out of a gallon bucket."

In the spring of 1984, a little over a decade after *Rodriguez* was handed down, some of the original plaintiffs, including Demetrio Rodriguez, along with more than sixty school districts, decided to once again challenge the Texas school financing system in court. This time, however, the litigants based their case on a different constitution, and brought their complaint to a different court. Since *Rodriguez* had effectively cut off appeal to the Equal Protection Clause in the U.S. Constitution, the challengers decided to rely on the equal protection language (no actual clause existed) in the Texas Constitution. The resulting case is known as *Edgewood v. Kirby* (1989).

Despite the doctrine of adequate and independent state grounds, it is sometimes the case that state courts allow federal understandings to guide interpretations of their own constitutions. There was no guarantee, therefore, that the Edgewood parents would be any more successful in state court than they had been in the federal system. Justice Powell's concern about the effect that equal distribution of educational resources might have on urban school districts, expressed throughout the *Rodriguez* deliberations, was no less relevant to state review than it had been to the federal courts. Powell knew that urban areas often had a large tax base that allowed them to spend more per pupil than could those in rural districts. In order to defeat this argument, courts would have to be convinced that *more* money is still not *enough* money, because the increase in dollars does not outweigh the increase in challenges faced by urban schools. Therefore, equal dollars do not lead to equal outcomes.

This debate between equality of input versus equality of output has been going on for quite some time. The Civil Rights Act of 1964, for example, required a study of educational inequality. The results were issued in 1966 in the form of a report entitled *Equality of Educational Opportunity*. This study has become known as "The Coleman Report" after its author, the sociologist James Coleman. To the shock and dismay of many reformers, the Coleman report demonstrated that there was little correlation between dollars spent on education and student outcomes. Instead, the study suggested that other factors, particularly the family background and socioeconomic status of the student, were a much better predictor of student success.

There are several ways to understand the results of the Coleman report. One way is to simply assume that money does not matter; that if one wants to equalize education, one has to equalize factors that are beyond the control of state legislatures. Others maintain that the problem is that different students have different needs; therefore, more, not equal, funding is needed in those communities that lack adequate family structures and supports. Nevertheless, although it may be obvious that students have different needs, converting those needs into a dollar amount is much more of a challenge.

In reaction to both the limitations put on equal protection jurisprudence by *Rodriguez* and the recognition that mere equality of spending might not improve education, litigants began to rely on language in their own state constitutions that went beyond basic equality concerns. They focused instead upon provisions (which exist in the constitutions of every state) mandating that a certain quality of education be provided by the legislature.

The school districts and parents who went to court in Texas in 1984 were no exception. Along with the provision in Article I of the Texas Constitution that "All men . . . have equal rights," they decided to rely on Article VII, section 1, which states: "A general diffusion of knowledge being essential to the preservation of the liberties and rights of the people, it shall be the duty of the Legislature of the State to establish and make suitable provision for the support and maintenance of an efficient system of public free schools."

In this and other cases, an important change took place in the legal and political discussions about school funding. Concerns about equity — or equal funding — were supplanted (at least partially) by arguments about adequacy. It is easy to see how this happened. The distinction between equity and adequacy is really just a shifting of focus from inputs to outputs. But since it is simpler to equalize dollar amounts placed into a system than it is to equalize student achievement, debates about the adequacy of an educational system almost always lead back to an examination of funding.

The state trial court, in which the new Texas lawsuit originated, agreed with the plaintiffs and concluded that both sections of the Texas Constitution had been violated. That decision, however, was overturned by a Texas court of appeals, which understood school funding to be a "political question" best suited for resolution by the governor and the state legislature. The case finally came before the Texas Supreme Court in 1989. The supreme court reversed the court of appeals, and, placing its decision squarely on the education provisions in Article VI of the Texas Constitution, held that "the state's school financing system is neither financially efficient nor efficient in the sense of providing for a 'general diffusion of knowledge' statewide." The court then promptly read the word "efficient" in the Texas Constitution to mean financial equality.

In an opinion that could have been written by Coons, Sugarman, and Clune, the Texas Supreme Court took judicial notice of the "glaring disparities" between the various school districts' abilities to raise money through property taxes. The justices seemed particularly distressed by the 700 to 1 difference in the property wealth available per student between the richest and poorest districts in Texas. Working backward, Justice Mauzy, who wrote for the court, began by connecting the resulting differences in school funding to the educational opportunities offered to the students in the poorest districts. He then declared that "children who live in the poor districts and children who live in rich districts must be afforded a substantially equal opportunity to have access to educational funds." He concluded by taking a swipe at Justice Powell's decision in *Rodriguez* and echoing Justice Marshall, arguing that the claim that school finance reform measures necessarily meant the end of local control "has no merit," since local control would only be enhanced if local school boards were given more funds with which to work.

The court's decision was stayed for seven months to give the Texas legislature time to act. Perhaps mindful of what had happened in *Rodriguez*, however, the court declared that if the Texas legislature failed to respond by May of the next year (1990), all state funding for public education would have to stop since the system had been found unconstitutional. Later, the trial court agreed to a brief extension of that deadline, and on June 7, 1990, the governor of Texas signed legislation that modified the school funding system. Senate Bill 1, as it became known, mandated fiscal neutrality for 95 percent of the school districts in Texas. That is, in all but the wealthiest 5 percent of the districts, there could be roughly no difference in the amount of money provided per student by local and state sources in districts that agreed to tax themselves at the same levels.

Senate Bill 1 was immediately challenged, and in January of 1991, the Supreme Court of Texas again found the system unconstitutional. Referring to Senate Bill 1 as a "Band-Aid," the court in *Edgewood II* admonished the legislature for ignoring the advantages of the wealthiest districts and leaving a system in place that, overall, allowed for extreme funding differences. Writing for the Texas court, Chief Justice Thomas Phillips made it clear that only a complete restructuring of the Texas school funding system, including perhaps the consolidation of the tax base of poor districts with rich districts, was likely to pass state constitutional muster. This time, the court gave the legislature only about three months to design a constitutional system.

The legislature responded, passing Senate Bill 351 in April of 1991. This bill achieved the financial consolidation of districts suggested by the court in *Edgewood II* through the creation of county education districts (CEDs). These were not, however, so much traditional school districts as they were taxing districts. Senate Bill 351 created a two-tiered funding system for education. Under tier one, each CED was required to levy a property tax sufficient to raise a specified amount of revenue for each student in the district. Within the second tier of school financing — beyond the basic amount mandated by tier one — the bill provided a form of fiscal neutrality. Each CED was guaranteed a specific amount of money (supplemented by the state, if necessary), for increases in the property tax rate beyond what was required under tier one. There was a cap, however, on how large a rate increase would be guaranteed by the state. The money raised by each CED would then be redistributed throughout the individual school districts within the larger county district.

One of the advantages of pursuing a case under a state constitution is that plaintiffs may find not only interpretations, but specific provisions that extend beyond anything found in the U.S. Constitution.

In *Edgewood III* (1991), however, those who wanted to reform the Texas school financing system discovered that this flexibility might prove to be a double-edged sword. In addition to the education provision already discussed, the Texas Constitution forbade the creation of a state property tax. After examining Senate Bill 351, the Supreme Court of Texas decided that because the taxes called for under the law were mandated by the state, they amounted to a state property tax. Moreover, Senate Bill 351 was found to be in violation of an additional section of the Texas Constitution because these taxes were to be instituted without prior approval from the voters who would have to pay the levies. Essentially, in attempting to comply with one section of the Texas Constitution, the legislature had run afoul of at least two other sections. This despite the fact that the same court, a few months earlier, had arguably suggested the precise remedy enacted by the state! This time, the court gave the legislature a year and a half to design a new school funding system.

The legislature's initial response to the Texas supreme court was to propose an amendment to the Texas Constitution that would have remedied the violations noted in *Edgewood III* and allowed for the creation of the CEDs. Given the racial subtext of the *Rodriguez* case, it is interesting to note that at least one study indicated that voting on the amendment paralleled racial divisions, with support for the amendment confined to African American and Mexican American communities. Ultimately, however, the amendment was soundly rejected. Following this defeat, the legislature went back to work, trying to craft a funding scheme that might somehow navigate between the constitutional responsibilities announced in *Edgewood I* and *Edgewood II* and the corresponding limitations imposed by the court in *Edgewood III*.

Finally, one month before the June 1993 deadline established by the court, the Texas legislature passed Senate Bill 7. Like the earlier school funding legislation, this bill created a two-tier funding system. Tier one provided a guaranteed per student funding level to any district that agreed to tax itself at a certain mandated rate ($.86 per $100 of property value). The second tier offered a form of district power equalization, with the state guaranteeing that increases in the property tax would yield a common minimum amount regardless of the amount of property wealth in a district. The difference between what was actually raised by the additional tax and the amount guaranteed by the law would be provided from the state's coffers. The total tax levied by a school district, however, could not exceed $1.50 per $100 of property value.

The distinction between Senate Bill 7 and the previous legislation was dubbed its "Robin Hood" feature. In *Edgewood III*, the Supreme Court of Texas had prevented the state from mandating a set property tax. Senate Bill 7 avoided state constitutional infirmity by setting voluntary minimum property tax rates. This is a typical approach governments use when trying to act outside of their delegated powers. For example, the U.S. Congress is not empowered by the Constitution to set a uniform speed limit or acceptable blood alcohol levels for drivers. The approach taken by Congress is to make the receipt of federal highway dollars contingent upon the "voluntary" acceptance of federal standards. This, incidentally, is the same approach taken by the federal government when it sets national education standards. Under Senate Bill 7, school districts in Texas wishing to collect state monies to supplement local property taxes had to tax themselves at a certain minimum level. Then, however, the legislation also provided for (once again voluntary) transfer of locally generated money from property rich districts to property poor districts. This goal was accomplished by providing districts with other options which, though constitutional, would most likely be considered unpalatable.

Specifically, the law capped each school district's maximum taxable property value per student at $208,000 (this amount was later increased). Any district whose wealth exceeded this amount was allowed to select from a menu of five possible options: (1) consolidate with another (poorer) district; (2) detach some of their property, thereby ceding some of the district's property wealth; (3) purchase average daily attendance credit from another district; (4) contract for the education of nonresident students; or (5) consolidate the district's tax base with a property-poor district. In a decision handed down in 1995 (*Edgewood IV*), the Texas Supreme Court found Senate Bill 7 constitutional. The matter is not settled, however. By 2002, the districts were back in court, and in November of 2004, a state judge once again ordered the legislature to restructure the Texas school finance system.

The case went before the Texas Supreme Court, and in November of 2005, that court once again declared the Texas funding system to be an unconstitutional imposition of a statewide tax.

## Other States

In support of his opinion in *Edgewood I*, Justice Mauzy concluded that his ruling was consistent with decisions handed down in other states. He had quite a bit of evidence on his side. In 1989, when *Edgewood I* was handed down, lawsuits challenging how schools were funded had been filed in Arkansas, California, Colorado, Connecticut, Kentucky, Georgia, Idaho, Maryland, Michigan, Montana, New Jersey, New York, Oklahoma, Oregon, Pennsylvania, South Carolina, Wisconsin, West Virginia, and Wyoming. In a majority of these states, the reformers met with at least limited success. This result encouraged many more such cases over the next decade.

There are two ways of looking at the phenomenon of judicial federalism. One could argue that the U.S. Supreme Court's decision to rule against Demetrio Rodriguez and his fellow litigants led to three decades of piecemeal litigation. Absent a federal constitutional requirement, reformers were forced to reargue their basic legal positions repeatedly in each state. The *Rodriguez* decision resulted in an enormous amount of legislative creativity, most — but not all — of which was driven by these state court decisions.

In a widely quoted dissenting opinion from 1932, Justice Louis Brandeis observed that "it is one of the happy accidents of the federal system that a single courageous state may, if its citizens choose, serve as a laboratory, and try novel social and economic experiments without risk to the rest of the country." School funding in the wake of *Rodriguez* has perhaps been the best example of both the virtue and the vice inherent in this "happy accident." Instead of a single national standard, states have been allowed to develop their own responses, prodded, if need be, by their own courts. Although it is true that a victory by *Rodriguez* in 1973 might have allowed the same differentiated state responses, the inertial pull toward federal control probably would have been irresistible. Those who advocate for more equality in educational opportunity have not been completely disappointed. Indeed, one such commentator has written that reading a history of the school funding cases made him "want to go out and hug a state court judge."

Obviously, it would take many thousands of words to explain what has happened in these other states. Some brief remarks about a few states, therefore, will have to suffice. It makes sense to start in California, since this is one of the states from which the school finance cases initially emerged.

## California

California found its reform efforts quickly squelched by a sort of "one-two punch." Initially, the state attempted to comply with the California Supreme Court's 1971 decision in *Serrano I* by passing legislation that approximately doubled the basic foundation amount guaranteed to each student. Still, since the plan did not provide for power equalization, enormous disparities in funding between school districts remained. In December of 1972, a trial court convened to hear evidence to determine whether the legislature's response was sufficient. In March of the next year, while the trial was still underway, the U.S. Supreme Court handed down *Rodriguez*. On the surface, the Supreme Court's decision dealt a devastating blow to the legal holding upon which the trial was based. After all, the California Supreme Court's finding in *Serrano I* that wealth was a suspect classification, and that there was a fundamental right to an education protected by the Fourteenth Amendment, was explicitly rejected by Justice Powell's majority opinion.

Nevertheless, when the California trial court delivered its decision in September of 1974, it was based squarely on *Serrano I*. How had the trial court preserved *Serrano I* in the face of *Rodriguez*? Depending upon your perspective, the reasoning was either ingenious or disingenuous. In *Serrano I*, the California Supreme Court had relied primarily on the Fourteenth Amendment. In a footnote to the opinion, however, the court concluded that California had also violated Article I, sections 11 and 21 of the California Constitution. This was because, in the words of the court (quoting in part a 1965 case), "We have construed these provisions [sections 11 and 21] as 'substantially the equivalent' of the equal protection clause of the Fourteenth Amendment to the federal Constitution." So, even though the Fourteenth Amendment had been pulled out from under the *Serrano I* decision, the California Constitution remained applicable.

Somewhat ironically, the court used Justice Powell's reasoning in *Rodriguez* to *reaffirm* the California Supreme Court's understanding of its own state constitution. The California trial court concluded that the interest children had in education was, in fact, "explicitly and implicitly guaranteed" by the California Constitution. Eventually, this line of reasoning was upheld by the California Supreme Court, which in *Serrano II* (1976) noted that although sections 11 and 21 of the California Constitution are "substantially the equivalent" of the Equal Protection Clause of the Fourteenth Amendment, they nevertheless "are possessed of an independent vitality." Relying upon this foundation, the court affirmed the trial court's determination that the legislative response to *Serrano I* had been inadequate.

For a time, therefore, it appeared that *Serrano* had survived *Rodriguez*. Indeed, following the court's decision in *Serrano II*, the California legislature passed Assembly Bill 65, which would have equalized school funding in California by implementing district power equalizing, redistributing property tax revenues from rich districts to poor districts.

Then came Proposition 13. Passed by referendum in 1978, Proposition 13 was an amendment to the California Constitution that limited property taxes to 1 percent of assessed value. At the same time, this amendment limited allowable increases to the assessed value of property and required a two-thirds vote in the state legislature to raise taxes. There is much debate among academics as to whether the *Serrano* cases "caused" Proposition 13. The result of Proposition 13, however, was clear. In the wake of limitations on local property tax revenues, the burden of funding the schools was placed more squarely on the shoulders of the state. The state legislature responded by developing a new funding system that relied more on state sources to fund the schools. At the same time, the state attempted to equalize funding in order to comply with the *Serrano* decisions. The result, certainly never intended by the original plaintiffs in the case, vindicated one of Justice Powell's concerns. School funding in California was leveled downward. Over time, this would lead California to go from being a state that provided some of the highest levels of funding per student to a state that was among those providing the least support.

## Ohio

Ohio might be able to lay claim to one of the oldest school funding cases. It began back in 1921, when Robert L. Miller refused to pay his property taxes, arguing that the levy violated both the federal and state constitutions. According to Ohio law at the time, the property tax was collected by the county, then redistributed to the various school districts within that county. Miller's specific complaint was that the property tax levied in the Silver Lake School District in which he resided was redistributed to other school districts throughout the county.

In *Miller v. Korns* (1923), the Supreme Court of Ohio ruled against Miller. The court relied upon Article VI, section 2 of the Ohio Constitution, which ordered the state legislature to "secure a thorough and efficient system of common schools throughout the state." In explaining what this clause meant, the court announced that "a thorough system could not mean one in which part of any number of school districts of the state were starved for funds. An efficient system could not mean one in which part of any number of school districts of the state lacked teachers, buildings, or equipment." This statement would later provide strong support for advocates of school funding reform in Ohio.

In April of 1976, the Cincinnati Board of Education, along with students and parents who lived in the school district of the city of Cincinnati, filed a class action suit claiming that Ohio's school funding system violated both the thorough and efficient clause (quoted above), and the equal protection and benefit clause of the Ohio Constitution. This latter clause states that "all political power is inherent in the People" and that this power is instituted for their "equal protection and benefit."

Ironically, Ohio had adopted exactly the remedy suggested by Coons, Sugarman, and Clune. In Ohio, as in some other states, property tax rates are referred to in terms of "mills." A mill is the equivalent of $1 for every $1,000 of assessed value. So, for example, a 1 mill assessment on property assessed at $10,000 would generate $10 in property tax revenue. The Ohio law challenged in this case guaranteed a yield of $48 per student per mill to any district willing to levy at least 20 mills of property tax. This equal yield formula would continue up to a maximum of 30 mills.

After hearing testimony for more than three months, the trial court ruled in favor of the plaintiffs and declared Ohio's school finance law in violation of both clauses in the state constitution. The decision was appealed, and the state court of appeals both affirmed and reversed the lower court. According to court of appeals, the school funding scheme was consistent with the demands of the thorough and efficient clause of the Ohio Constitution. Nevertheless, the funding scheme was found to be in violation of the equal protection and benefit clause. The final word, of course, would come from the Ohio Supreme Court.

In June of 1979, the Ohio Supreme Court issued its opinion in *Cincinnati v. Walter*. Although this decision, and the case itself, was based only on the Ohio Constitution, the U.S. Supreme Court's decision in *Rodriguez* was front and center. When applying the equal protection and benefit clause of the Ohio Constitution, the court of appeals had used the same two-tiered approach traditionally used in Fourteenth Amendment equal protection cases. Justice Brown wrote for the majority on the Ohio Supreme Court and acknowledged that, based on the understanding of that test put forth in *Rodriguez*, the court of appeals was correct in its decision, since education is a right "explicitly or implicitly" recognized by the Ohio Constitution. Nevertheless, Justice Brown explained, the *Rodriguez* test was not applicable in this case because the two-tiered standard only applied to equal protection challenges arising under the U.S. Constitution. In applying the equal protection guarantees of the Ohio Constitution, the proper standard was a version of the rational basis test under which a court would determine whether a state's actions were unconstitutional "beyond a reasonable doubt." In this case such a showing had not been made.

The supreme court then moved to an examination of whether the thorough and efficient clause had been violated. After quoting favorably the language from *Miller v. Korns* mentioned previously, Justice Brown returned to *Rodriguez*. Recall that Justice Powell, in distinguishing *Rodriguez* from cases involving ballot access, argued that the Texas funding scheme did not result in the "absolute deprivation of education." The Ohio court concluded that the essential lesson of

*Miller* was similar to that of *Rodriguez:* Only the absolute deprivation of education to students would be viewed as a constitutional violation. In the words of the Ohio Supreme Court, "The fact that a better financing system could be devised which would be more efficient or more thorough is not material."

This is the way things remained until 1994, when a group calling itself the Ohio Coalition for Equity and Adequacy of School Funding went to court in rural Perry County on behalf of a high school student named Nathan DeRolph. Although there had been no serious school funding litigation in Ohio since 1979, the state had, by this time, modified its school funding laws. Reflecting the national movement from equity to adequacy, Ohio, in 1980, dropped its power equalizing plan and moved to a foundation system. The state would first determine a minimum "foundation" amount guaranteed to each student. Then, the state would provide the difference between the foundation amount and the revenue that the local school district could provide through property taxes. The formula amount was essentially determined by a backward calculation after the state had concluded how much state money would be available for primary and secondary education during the two-year period covered by each state budget.

In what could only be called a wide-ranging decision, Judge Linton Lewis, the trial court judge who first heard *DeRolph v. State of Ohio* (1997), decided that, since Ohio was no longer funding its schools the way it did in 1979, *Walter* was no longer a binding precedent. Judge Lewis then declared that education was a fundamental right in Ohio and applied the strict scrutiny standard, concluding that local control over schools was not a compelling state interest. Finally, the judge announced that Ohio's system of school funding violated the thorough and efficient clause of the state constitution.

At first, it appeared as if the state would not appeal the trial court's decision. Eventually, however, the decision was contested, and in August of 1995, the court of appeals, relying on *Walter,* reversed most of the trial court's decision. Almost two years later, in March of 1997, the Ohio Supreme Court finally issued an opinion in what became known as *DeRolph I.*

In *DeRolph I,* the Ohio Supreme Court partially overturned the court of appeals, and found that the State of Ohio violated the thorough and efficient clause. The court agreed that *Walter* was not applicable, and instead cited the Texas Supreme Court's (*Edgewood I*) interpretation of what constituted "efficiency" in school funding. Of course, the Ohio Supreme Court also relied on the language from *Miller.* The Ohio Supreme Court was most disturbed by the fact that the foundation amount had "absolutely no connection with what is necessary to provide each district with enough money to ensure an adequate educational program." Its conclusion was that the funding system would have to undergo "a complete systematic overhaul."

In response to *DeRolph I,* the Ohio legislature enacted several laws designed to change how that state's schools were funded. Although still maintaining a basic foundation approach (renamed "basic state aid"), the legislature calculated this amount by looking to the average amount spent per student by districts meeting seventeen out of eighteen performance criteria, which were basically measures of how well school districts were accomplishing their educational mission.

Ohio merged traditional input measures (funding amounts) with output measures (performance). Still, the link between outputs and inputs was far from perfect, since, in arriving at the average, the legislature had screened out the top and bottom ten percent (in terms of the amount spent per student) of the high-performing districts. Moreover, the increased foundational amount was scheduled to be phased in over a number of years.

In *DeRolph II* (2000) the Ohio Supreme Court examined each of the legislative remedies and offered its own definition of what constitutes a thorough and efficient system of educational funding. According to the court, such a system is one in which each school district "has enough funds to operate . . . has ample number of teachers . . . and equipment sufficient for all students to be afforded an educational opportunity." The Ohio court then concluded that, although progress had been made, the legislature had fallen short of the "complete systematic overhaul" demanded by *DeRolph I.*

The Ohio legislature reacted to the supreme court by passing House Bill 94. This legislation established twenty-seven performance standards and then used the average per student spending in districts that met twenty of these standards to determine the foundation (base cost) amount. This average, however, was determined by using "wealth screens" that eliminated the wealthiest and poorest 5 percent of the districts. Rounding was used when determining which districts met the performance standards, and this led to inclusion of a few districts that passed only eighteen or nineteen of the twenty-seven measures.

The phase-in period that had been criticized in *DeRolph II* was eliminated, and a new category of spending called parity aid was added. Parity aid is a form of power equalizing that applies to property tax millage in poorer districts beyond that required to fulfill the local contribution to the base amount.

The Ohio Supreme Court's response to these changes in *DeRolph III* (2001) was controversial even among the justices. Chief Justice Thomas Moyer, who wrote for the court, went beyond merely finding the response inadequate, and instead suggested how the legislation might be altered in a way that would render it constitutional. Despite the court's earlier command to conduct a "complete overhaul" of the system, the opinion gave conditional approval to the state's retaining a basic foundation approach and ordered the legislature to recalculate the foundation amount without rounding and without using the wealth screens. Essentially, the Ohio Supreme Court designed a school funding plan that would meet their criteria for a thorough and efficient system. Although there was some disagreement over precisely how much the supreme court's plan would cost the state, the demand for the increase could not have come at a worse time. An economic downturn had decreased tax revenues and made balancing the state budget an increasingly difficult proposition.

The state quickly asked the court to reconsider its opinion, and after a mediator assigned by the supreme court failed to reach agreement between the parties, a fourth *DeRolph* opinion was produced. In *DeRolph IV* (2003), a majority of the Ohio Supreme Court announced that they had changed their "collective mind." The plan set forth in *DeRolph III* was vacated, and the supreme court reaffirmed its holding in the first two decisions (*DeRolph I* and *Derolph II*). Because the court did not retain jurisdiction in the case, however, *DeRolph IV* ended more than five years of litigation without any resolution. The court had made a declaration, but, unlike in Texas, no injunction was issued. In May of 2003, about five months after its decision in *DeRolph IV,* the Ohio Supreme Court granted the state's request to end any further litigation in the *DeRolph* matter (*State ex rel. State v. Lewis*).

The manner in which the Ohio cases ended sheds light on yet another legacy of *Rodriguez*. Frustrated with what they saw as a failure by the state to remedy a state funding system that had been found unconstitutional, the *DeRolph* plaintiffs petitioned the U.S. Supreme Court. In a footnote to their brief, the petitioners stated that they were not seeking a reconsideration of *Rodriguez*. Nevertheless, in a later footnote, they offered that the Court "may view this case as an opportunity to reconsider the fundamentality of education." In their response brief, asking the Supreme Court to deny certiorari in the case, Ohio argued that "*Rodriguez* has ensured that states may work out their own approaches to education." Ultimately, the U.S. Supreme Court declined to review the case.

# CHAPTER 11

# Constitutional Legacy

In addition to all of the state education cases that resulted indirectly from *Rodriguez*, there is another legacy that should not be omitted. *Rodriguez* contained major legal holdings that influenced future cases decided regarding the Fourteenth Amendment. Justice Powell's opinion declared that individuals do not enjoy a fundamental right to an education. In addition, the majority opinion announced that state classifications based on wealth were not "suspect" in a constitutional sense. The result was that *Rodriguez* removed a legal burden from the backs of the states. When it came to educational funding, the legal presumption would be that whatever the state did was constitutional, at least under the federal document. More broadly, however, the same presumption would be in place in the event that government action created any distinctions between the poor and the wealthy.

It is easy to overstate this conclusion, however. In *Rodriguez*, the Court recognized the importance of — and perhaps even a nonfundamental right to — education, as well as the fact that some distinctions between wealthy and poor students did exist. The result was that a test — the rational basis standard — was applied. States may not indiscriminately violate rights, nor may they arbitrarily assign goods to different individuals. Some reasoned or rational basis must lie behind the government's actions. This led to a final important holding in *Rodriguez:* A state's interest in local control over education was of sufficient importance to counterbalance any equal protection concerns. In legal terms, the state had a legitimate interest in maintaining local control over the schools. Of the various holdings, this assertion of the importance of local control would have the most immediate impact.

## Milliken v. Bradley

In February of 1974, less than a year after *Rodriguez* was decided, the Court heard arguments in a dispute involving a plan for interdistrict busing in the Detroit metropolitan area. Four years earlier, in an effort to achieve desegregation goals, the Detroit Board of Education adopted a plan under which high school students would be bused across school district lines. The Michigan legislature quickly passed legislation that prevented the implementation of the plan, and the Detroit branch of the NAACP reacted by seeking an injunction against that legislation.

The resulting case, *Milliken v. Bradley* (1974), like *Rodriguez*, is best understood in the context of the Court's earlier decision in *Brown v. Board of Education*. Although *Brown* addressed legal (de jure) segregation, *Milliken* involved segregation as a matter of fact or deed (de facto).

The only way to cure de facto segregation, short of making people live in a particular area, is to order students to go to schools outside of their neighborhoods. This almost always involves busing; and that was certainly the case in Detroit. But this was not unusual: busing students to new schools in order to achieve greater integration was occurring all over the country and the Supreme Court had, in previous terms, given guarded approval to the practice. The *Milliken* case differed, however, in that it involved busing *across* district lines. In resolving the issue, the district court had ordered the implementation of a desegregation plan that included a majority of the suburban districts surrounding Detroit.

In a five to four decision, the same majority that upheld the Texas school funding system in *Rodriguez* voted together to overturn the Detroit desegregation plan. This time, however, Powell did not draft the majority opinion. Instead, Chief Justice Burger retained the opinion for himself. Nevertheless, Justice Powell's opinion in *Rodriguez* was woven into Burger's logic. The chief justice wrote that if the desegregation plan went forward, the result would be the "consolidation of 54 independent school districts historically administered as separate units into a vast super school district." Without *Rodriguez*, this situation might have been seen as merely a historical trend on par with overturning the tradition of legal segregation in *Brown*. In *Rodriguez*, however, Justice Powell had raised the principle of local control over schools to constitutional status. This interest in local control might be overcome, but the state would have to demonstrate that it was remedying some larger constitutional violation. For example, in *Rodriguez*, if a fundamental right to an education had been identified, and if the realization of that right was thwarted by an unequal funding system, then the interest in local control could be overcome. In *Milliken*, Burger was unable to find a counterbalancing right that had been violated, since the suburban districts had never imposed legal segregation on black students. If the outlying districts had not participated in violating anyone's constitutional rights, why, Burger wondered, should they be required to abandon their interest in local control?

One might speculate about how the chief justice would have assembled his logic absent Justice Powell's earlier opinion. What harm, beyond perhaps a slightly longer bus trip, would white students have suffered if required to attend schools outside of their local district? Powell's heartfelt — and apparently earnest — protests in *Rodriguez* about the importance of local school boards gave those who opposed interdistrict busing an argument that otherwise might have lacked power.

The link between *Rodriguez* and *Milliken* goes beyond Chief Justice Burger's majority opinion. In dissent, Justice Douglas also relied on the prior year's case. Echoing *Hobson*, Douglas observed that there was a link between race and poverty, since blacks tended to be poorer than whites. The promise of *Brown v. Board of Education* had been equal educational opportunities. In *Rodriguez*, however, unequal funding between rich and poor districts had been given the stamp of constitutional approval. But, Douglas argued, if poor school districts and districts with a high percentage of minorities were one and the same, and minority districts could not be judicially merged with nonminority districts, then an end-run around *Brown* had been discovered. Although it was true that black students would receive different educational opportunities because of where they lived, and not because of the color of their skin, the end result differed little from the racial inequality of educational opportunities forbidden by *Brown*. Indeed, for Douglas the Court's decision in *Milliken* harkened back to days well before *Brown* was decided. He wrote that, "So far as equal protection is concerned, we are now in a dramatic retreat from the 7-to-1 decision in 1896 that blacks could be segregated in public facilities, provided they received equal treatment."

Douglas referred to *Plessy v. Ferguson*, the 1896 case that was overturned by the decision in *Brown*. In *Plessy*, the Supreme Court announced the doctrine of "separate but equal." Under this doctrine, segregation laws did not run afoul of the equal protection guarantees of the Fourteenth Amendment unless it could be shown that the facilities provided to one race were inferior to those provided to another. Because the NAACP wanted the Supreme Court to explicitly overturn *Plessy* in *Brown*, they brought challenges from school districts where states had spent considerable funds trying to equalize segregated schools. Therefore, the Court determined the inequality in segregated schools to be the result of the stigma inherent in the segregation laws themselves and not of the disparities between the schools. In his dissent in *Milliken*, Douglas implied that the Court had granted its imprimatur to a situation that need not even meet the discredited separate but equal standard from *Plessy*.

―――――

## *Maher v. Roe*

Although *Rodriguez* most directly affected cases involving education, its influence was far-reaching. To understand why this is so, it is necessary to remember that there is a difference between courts and legislatures. The reasoning-by-example process that is fundamental to judicial decisionmaking means that every opinion, particularly by the U.S. Supreme Court, has the potential to influence a whole line of cases — or even several lines of cases — that might come before courts at some future date. The only requirement is that the future cases share some arguable elements of either fact or law (or both) with the proposed precedent. *Rodriguez* involved legal questions that were severable from the actual facts of the case. Taken broadly, *Rodriguez* offered instruction to future courts faced with challenges on which a party alleges a violation of a right that is not specifically enumerated within the text of the Constitution. Moreover, insofar as the *Rodriguez* challenge was based squarely on the Fourteenth Amendment's Equal Protection Clause, it had the potential to guide cases brought under that constitutional provision whether or not they involved education. This, indeed, is what occurred.

On October 11, 1972, the day before *Rodriguez* was argued before the Supreme Court, the Court heard rearguments in the abortion case known as *Roe v. Wade* (1973). Of course, *Roe* would become an even more controversial case than *Rodriguez*, although, as matter of law, not necessarily a more significant one. In the spring of 1973, when both *Rodriguez* and *Roe* were handed down, however, few might have anticipated the impact that the former case would have on the latter. Nevertheless, the two cases would come together four years later, when the Court decided *Maher v. Roe* (1977).

In the wake of the Court's decision in *Roe v. Wade*, many states passed laws that attempted to limit or regulate the practice of abortion within the guidelines set down by Justice Blackmun's majority decision. For example, in 1975, the Connecticut Welfare Department issued a regulation limiting Medicaid funding of abortion procedures. Under the regulation, only abortions that were deemed medically necessary would be subsidized by Medicaid payments. This regulation was challenged by two poor women who argued that they were unable to fund their own abortions. Since the procedures were, in these cases, not deemed medically necessary, the women had no recourse but to continue their pregnancies. A three-judge district court ruled against the regulations, and the state appealed to the Supreme Court.

Justice Powell wrote for the Court. The six-member majority included all of the justices who had joined Powell in *Rodriguez*. John Paul Stevens, whom President Gerald Ford had nominated to replace the retiring Justice Douglas, provided the sixth vote.

*Maher* shared more with *Rodriguez* than common authorship. This was not unexpected, since the claims made by the appellants in *Maher* mirrored those that had been rejected in *Rodriguez*. First, the plaintiffs asserted that the Medicaid regulation resulted in inequality between rich women, who could afford to pay for their own abortions, and poor women, who would not be able to rely on Medicaid payments to cover the same procedures.

Powell began his opinion by arguing that the "basic framework of analysis of such a claim is well settled." Quoting extensively from his opinion in *Rodriguez*, he concluded that Connecticut had not discriminated against a suspect class. Of course, this does not dispose of the claim, but instead indicates that the state will be able to justify its regulation merely by showing that it is advancing a legitimate state interest. As Powell then explained, however, this would not be the case, and a higher standard would apply, if the Connecticut regulation violated a fundamental right, which, Powell defined, once again quoting from *Rodriguez*, as a right "explicitly or implicitly protected by the Constitution."

The influence of the earlier case was most profound, in fact, when Powell began to examine this latter claim. In *Rodriguez*, although citing precedents that might have determined whether poor children in Texas had been denied their fundamental right to an education, Powell had observed that the cases in which the Court had found that fundamental right had been infringed upon all involved the kind of "absolute deprivation of a desired benefit" that was different from the mere underfunding of schools. Powell carried this line of reasoning into his *Maher* opinion and, indeed, into his interpretation of the fundamental right recognized by *Roe v. Wade* (1973).

A year earlier, Justice Blackmun, the author of *Roe*, had suggested laws that regulated abortion were only unconstitutional if they placed "undue burdens" on that right. In *Maher*, Powell seized upon this language. By failing to provide funding for abortion, Connecticut had clearly made it more difficult for poor women to exercise that choice. As in *Rodriguez*, however, although the right was clearly burdened, there was no absolute deprivation. Poor women could still obtain abortions if they could somehow manage to find the funds. As he had in *Rodriguez*, therefore, Powell concluded that since there was no "unduly burdensome interference" upon a right, the state merely had to show that the regulation was related to its legitimate interest. In *Maher*, Powell found that promoting childbirth was just such an interest.

Within the long line of abortion cases that appeared on the Court's docket fairly regularly between 1973 and 1992, *Maher* seemed relatively insignificant. It might have been, had not Powell's (and, at least for a time, Blackmun's) argument been picked up six years later by Justice Sandra Day O'Connor when she dissented in *Akron v. Akron Center for Reproductive Health* (1983). Ironically, O'Connor was dissenting from a majority opinion authored by Justice Powell in which he explained why abortion regulations promulgated by the city of Akron, Ohio, were unconstitutional.

That Powell even wrote for the Court in the *Akron* case is interesting. He was part of a six-member majority including Justices Brennan and Marshall (dissenters in *Rodriguez*), along with Justice John Paul Stevens, Justice Blackmun, and, oddly enough, Chief Justice Burger.

Although Burger had signed onto *Roe*, his discomfort with that decision had quickly become apparent. Therefore, it was unusual to find Burger in the majority on a decision that overturned an abortion regulation based on the argument that it ran afoul of *Roe*.

When he served as chief justice, Burger was accused by his fellow justices of joining majorities on the Court simply to make sure that he controlled the eventual assignment of the majority opinion. One can make a strong argument that this is precisely what happened in *Akron*. Powell's earlier decision in the Connecticut case might have led Burger to believe he could rely on Powell to deliver a rather narrow statement overturning the Akron ordinance. This, of course, would limit the usefulness of *Akron* as a precedent for future abortion cases.

Regardless of what Burger expected, Powell delivered an opinion unreserved in its support of *Roe*. Indeed, Powell's reasoning in *Akron* was hard to reconcile with what he had written six years earlier. Outside of a general footnote citing virtually all of the abortion cases that followed *Roe*, Powell failed to even mention *Maher* or the undue burden standard. In fact, Powell's opinion relied on fairly traditional equal protection analysis, threaded through the trimester formula first articulated by Justice Blackmun in *Roe*.

Dissenting in *Akron*, Justice O'Connor argued that this was the wrong standard. Her authority for this position was Powell's opinion in *Maher*. She even quoted Justice Powell's opinion in that case, asserting: "Our recent cases indicate that a regulation imposed on a lawful abortion is not unconstitutional unless it unduly burdens that right to an abortion" (internal quotations omitted).

By 1992, when O'Connor joined with Justices Souter and Kennedy in a joint opinion upholding almost all of Pennsylvania's abortion statute (which was very similar to the Akron law overturned almost a decade earlier), the undue burden standard had become the legal test for determining whether such regulations were constitutional. Although Powell himself was off the Court by this time, his earlier opinion in *Rodriguez* helped pave the way for what has become the dominant legal approach in abortion cases.

# CHAPTER 12

# Conclusion

According to a 1997 U.S. Government Accounting Office (GAO) report entitled *School Finance: State Efforts to Reduce Funding Gaps between Poor and Wealthy Districts*, wealthy school districts were able to spend 24 percent more per student than poorer districts. The report shows how much of an influence the Coons team had on how we think about school funding. Among other measures, the GAO calculated a fiscal neutrality score, which represented how much the total income of individuals within a school district correlated with per student spending on education. Of the forty-nine states examined in the study (Hawaii, which has only one statewide school district was omitted), thirty-seven had a positive fiscal neutrality score; that is, school spending increased along with local income. Texas, however, was among the twelve states in which the correlation was either zero or negative. After thirty years and at least four major court battles, much has changed, at least in Texas.

Across the nation, large disparities in the amount of money available per student still exist. In part, this is because of the holding in *Rodriguez* denying a federal remedy in educational funding cases. Also, however, the nation has moved away from focusing strictly on funding, and instead has begun paying more attention to results or outputs. This is commonly known as the movement from equity to adequacy, and is reflected in the popularity of proficiency tests: they provide at least a rough measure of how effective schools are at achieving their central mission of educating students. There is some reason to believe that the relationship between equal funding and equal outcomes is tenuous, if it exists at all. Take, for example, the Edgewood and Alamo Heights Independent School Districts, the two school districts that were at the center of the *Rodriguez* case.

In 1968, when Arthur Gochman filed the case on behalf of Demetrio Rodriguez and the other Edgewood parents, affidavits were gathered showing the revenue gap between the impoverished Edgewood School District and the wealthier Alamo Heights School District. During the 1967–1968 school year, Alamo Heights was able to spend $594 per pupil, and Edgewood could only raise $356 for each of their students. Under the so-called Robin Hood system in Texas, that gap has disappeared. Indeed, the Edgewood School District now has a $1,000 per student advantage over the Alamo Heights School District. This is entirely the result of state spending; the State of Texas now provides almost 78 percent of the money spent in Edgewood. Alamo Heights, on the other hand, must provide almost 90 percent of its revenue from local taxes. Looking at these numbers, it is easy to argue that Texas has remedied its equity problem. But has the adequacy problem been solved?

Beginning in 2003, the State of Texas began using the Texas Assessment of Knowledge and Skills (TAKS) to evaluate the performance of its public school system. The tests are administered to students in grades three through eleven and measure competencies in areas such as reading, writing, and mathematics and, in the later grades, science and social studies. On average across all grades, 50 percent of Edgewood students met the TAKS standards in 2004. Compare this number to Alamo Heights, where 85 percent of students met these same standards, although the wealthier district had less revenue available. Obviously, equalizing money does not equalize results.

In looking back over the past three decades, education and its relationship to wealth and especially race has remained at the center of national political debates; yet with the passage of the Educational and Secondary Act of 2001 (usually referred to as No Child Left Behind [NCLB]), things appear to have come full circle. Critics and proponents of that controversial act would agree that No Child Left Behind increases the federal presence in education. That the act itself speaks in terms of outputs rather than inputs shows how far the debate has evolved since 1973. Those who see in NCLB an underfunded federal mandate are perhaps inadvertently resurrecting both sides of the *Rodriguez* debate. Critics argue that the results cannot be achieved unless more money is provided to the schools. At the same time there is hostility to the very notion of federal guidelines superceding local control over educational decisions. The fact that this debate goes on mainly in Congress and the state legislatures and in state rather than federal courts speaks volumes about the continued impact of Powell's decision in *Rodriguez*.

More generally, it is impossible for anyone to grasp the scope of the Fourteenth Amendment without understanding *Rodriguez*. In this way, Arthur Gochman was right. Soon after he brought the case, Gochman concluded that he would probably lose in the Supreme Court because the Court's makeup had changed. The Warren Court, with its expansive view of the Fourteenth Amendment, could not survive the resignation of four of its members. Ironically, Powell, who replaced Hugo Black, represented the smallest change from his predecessor.

In retrospect, it makes perfect sense that Powell would have had Larry Hammond, Black's former clerk, draft the initial opinion in *Rodriguez*. Within the annals of Supreme Court history, Black stands out as a voice against those who move beyond the plain words of the Constitution. Prior to being appointed to the Court by Franklin Roosevelt, Black had been one of the leaders behind FDR's 1937 plan to "pack" the Supreme Court with justices who shared Roosevelt's constitutional philosophy. The purpose of the plan was to rein in a Court that had, in Roosevelt's view, moved far beyond the Constitution.

Although known as a great champion of civil rights and civil liberties — Black was, after all, the justice who held the bible when Thurgood Marshall took his oath and became the first African American to serve on the nation's highest court — the former senator did little to hide his disdain for many of the Warren Court's later decisions.

Speaking toward the end of his tenure on the Court, Black singled out one of the most famous (or infamous) Warren Court decisions, *Griswold v. Connecticut* (1965), for criticism. Over the strongly worded objections of Justice Black, Justice Douglas had in that case argued that married couples enjoyed a right to privacy under the "penumbras, formed by emanations" from various specific guarantees in the Bill of Rights. In his speech, entitled "The Role of Courts in Our Constitutional System," Justice Black, although acknowledging that he personally valued privacy, insisted that he could "find in the Constitution no language which either specifically or implicitly grants to all individuals a constitutional 'right to privacy.'" Black was not so much criticizing Douglas's result as his method. In looking to "penumbras, from emanations," Douglas had failed to restrict himself to that which is "specifically or implicitly" mentioned in the document. For Black, such limitations were crucial if judges were not to become legislators.

Powell, Black's successor on the Court, shared these sympathies. In *Rodriguez*, he argued that judges must, when searching for fundamental rights in the Constitution, confine themselves to that which is "explicitly or implicitly guaranteed" by the document itself. In a letter to his former law clerk, J. Harvie Wilkinson, III, Powell wrote that "one of the virtues of *Rodriguez* is that — although its analysis followed the prevailing law at the time — the opinion did place limits on the then trend toward revolving door expansion of fundamental rights." This had, apparently, always been his view of the *Rodriguez* case. Indeed, on the Saturday before oral argument in *Rodriguez*, Powell concluded a sixteen-page memo to Hammond by writing that he often reminded himself that "we are not a superlegislature, that judicial restraint is a cardinal virtue when approaching an issue of constitutionality." In this he followed very much the philosophy of Larry Hammond's former boss, Justice Black.

And so in the end, *Rodriguez* provides many possible legacies. Proponents of the Court's decision find in this case a powerful statement in support of both federalism and judicial restraint. Critics argue that *Rodriguez* was a missed opportunity to expand on *Brown v. Board of Education* and declare, once and for all, a constitutionally protected right to an education. What is not in doubt, however, is that *Rodriguez* left a strong and distinctive imprint upon U.S. constitutional law.

# Epilogue
## Por Que, Por Que

Driving into San Antonio on a bright, sunny morning, I was eagerly anticipating my meeting with Demetrio Rodriguez. I had already been reading and writing about this case for more than a year, and had developed an odd sense of familiarity with the major players in the case. Having sifted through the records at the Lewis Powell archives, for example, and seeing the many memos addressed "Dear Larry" (Larry Hammond, the law clerk who worked on the *Rodriguez* case with Justice Powell) and "Dear Jay" (for then Powell law clerk and now Court of Appeals judge J. Harvie Wilkinson, III), I felt as if I knew these individuals, albeit circa the early 1970s.

But Demetrio Rodriguez was different. I had typed the word "Rodriguez" (underlined to denote the name of a legal case) many times, but the man himself was more of an abstraction. From newspaper interviews published when the case was first decided, and Peter Irons's work, I knew something of his background. But I was curious about his personality.

Mr. Rodriguez still lives in the poor Edgewood section of San Antonio, filled with small one-story houses squeezed together and surrounded by low, chain-linked fences. There was nothing that distinguished his house from all the others. He even had the obligatory "beware of dog" sign that seemed to be hung on every other fence (although the only dog I saw was a small beagle that seemed unaware that a stranger was present).

When I arrived at his house, Mr. Rodriguez was waiting in his yard. It occurred to me that he seemed as eager to meet me as I was to meet him. As we sat down in his living room, he spoke easily and proudly about his past, his parents, and his children. Then, in response to a question from me about why he had decided to get involved in this litigation, he laughed and told me that, when he was younger, friends and family would tease him by calling him "por que, por que," Spanish for "why, why." Anyone who spent more than five minutes with Mr. Rodriguez would harbor no doubts about the appropriateness of that nickname. Although I was there to interview him, he seemed as interested in listening as he was in talking. Indeed, about halfway through the conversation, he turned the tables on me and began posing his own questions. "Why," he asked, "can't we solve this school problem? Why can't we give the schools the money that they need?"

I tried to answer, talking about the various interests involved and how legislatures are nervous about offending voters, upsetting long-established systems, and having to raise taxes. I also touched upon the fact that the correlation between school funding and school quality had never been conclusively demonstrated. Although I suspect he was not satisfied with my responses, he clearly enjoyed talking about the issue. At seventy-eight years of age, this man who had never moved beyond the tenth grade wanted to learn. Indeed, I found his curiosity both infectious and inspiring.

As I have explained earlier in this book, it is something of an accident that Rodriguez's name appears at the top of this case. As Demetrio Rodriguez readily admits, he was no more important than any of the other six people who had signed onto the lawsuit. There is a temptation to overly personalize a case like this to give it a more human face. I would like to think, however, that Demetrio Rodriguez is an apt representative of all of the litigants. Like the others, Demetrio Rodriguez was unwilling to accept a system that he thought was unfair. He — they — demanded that the state of Texas explain "why" this inequality existed.

They made a difference. As I was leaving Mr. Rodriguez's home, I noticed a wall full of plaques and awards from various groups. As I read the inscriptions, I noticed that one of the awards belonged not to Demetrio Rodriguez but to his daughter Patricia. When I asked about it, Mr. Rodriguez proudly shared with me that his daughter was a teacher and had been named "teacher of year" at the school where she worked. As it turned out, she worked in the same Edgewood School District that Demetrio Rodriguez and others had fought so hard to improve thirty years earlier. Quite a legacy.

| | |
|---|---|
| 1839 | Congress of the Republic of Texas parcels off land in each county to be used for public schools |
| 1845 | Texas is admitted to the union as a state; first state constitution calls for the legislature "to establish free schools throughout the state of Texas" |
| 1854 | School districts are established in Texas |
| 1875 | First public schools are created |
| 1876 | Texas Constitution set aside 25 percent of occupational tax and poll tax to support public schools |
| 1948 | Gilmer-Aiken Committee, half made up of legislators and half members of the general public, proposes the Texas Minimum Foundation Program |
| 1965 | Governor John Connally creates the Governor's Committee on Public School Education |
| 1967 | *Hobson v. Hanson* decided in the District of Columbia |
| March 31, 1968 | President Lyndon Johnson announces he will not seek reelection |
| June 1968 | Chief Justice Earl Warren announces his retirement |
| July 30, 1968 | *San Antonio v. Rodriguez* filed in federal district court for the Western District of Texas |
| November 15, 1968 | *McInnis v. Shapiro* decided (D.C.) |
| January 1969 | Three-judge district court impaneled to hear *Rodriguez* |
| May 14, 1969 | Abe Fortas resigns |
| May 23, 1969 | *Burruss v. Wilkerson* decided (D.C.) |
| June 23, 1969 | Warren Burger sworn in as chief justice |
| June 9, 1970 | Harry Blackmun replaces Justice Fortas |
| January–June 1971 | Texas legislative session |
| August 30, 1971 | California Supreme Court hands down *Serrano v. Priest* |
| September 1971 | Justices Hugo Black and John Marshall Harlan announce their retirements |

| | |
|---|---|
| October 1971 | depositions begin in *Rodriguez* |
| December 23, 1971 | Three-judge district court hands down its decision in *Rodriguez* |
| January 7, 1972 | Lewis F. Powell replaces Justice Hugo Black; William H. Rehnquist replaces Justice John Marshall Harlan |
| January 26, 1972 | Three-judge district court issues a clarification to its *Rodriguez* opinion |
| April 17, 1972 | Texas files appeal with the Supreme Court |
| June 7, 1972 (last day of 1971 session) | Supreme Court announces its decision to note probable jurisdiction in *Rodriguez* |
| October 12, 1972 | Oral arguments heard in *Rodriguez* |
| March 21, 1973 | Supreme Court issues its decision in *Rodriguez* |
| December 30, 1976 | California Supreme Court issues *Serrano II* |
| October 2, 1989 | Texas Supreme Court decides against the state in *Edgewood v. Kirby* |

# CASES CITED

*Aetna v. Weber Casualty and Surety Co.*, 406 U.S. 164 (1972)

*Akron v. Akron Center for Reproductive Health*, 462 U.S. 416 (1983)

*Bolling v. Sharpe*, 347 U.S. 497 (1954)

*Brown v. Board of Education*, 347 U.S. 483 (1954)

*Bullock v. Carter*, 405 U.S. 134 (1972)

*Burruss v. Wilkerson*, 310 F. Supp. 572 (1969), aff'd 397 U.S. 44 (1970)

*Cincinnati v. Walter*, 58 Ohio St. 2d 368 (1979)

*Columbia Broadcasting v. Democratic National Committee*, 412 U.S. 94 (1973)

*Craig v. Boren*, 429 U.S. 190 (1976)

*Cummings v. Board of Education of Richmond County*, 175 U.S. 528 (1899)

*Dandridge v. Williams*, 397 U.S. 471 (1970)

*Davis v. School Board of Prince Edward County*, 347 U.S. 483 (1954)

*Delgado v. Bastrop Independent School District*, Civ. No. 388 (W.D. Tex. June 15, 1948)

*DeRolph v. State of Ohio*
    78 Ohio St. 3d 193 (1997) (*DeRolph I*)
    89 Ohio St. 3d 1 (2000) (*DeRolph II*)
    93 Ohio St. 3d 309 (2001) (*DeRolph III*)
    97 Ohio St. 3d 434 (2002) (*DeRolph IV*)

*Edgewood Independent School District, et al., Petitioners v. Kirby*
    777 S.W. 2d 391 (1989) (*Edgewood I*)
    804 S.W. 2d 491 (1991) (*Edgewood II*)
    34 Tex. Sup. J 368 (1991) (*Edgewood III*)
    893 S.W. 2d 450 (1995) (*Edgewood IV*)

*Food Employees v. Logan Valley Plaza*, 391 U.S. 308 (1968)

*Furman v. Georgia*, 408 U.S. 238 (1972)

*Griffin v. Prince Edward County*, 377 U.S. 218 (1964)

*Griswold v. Connecticut*, 381 U.S. 479 (1965)

*Guerra v. Smith*, No. 71-2857 (1969) aff'd 474 F.2d 1399 (1973)

*Harper v. Virginia Board of Elections*, 383 U.S. 663 (1966)

*Hawkins v. Town of Shaw*, 437 F. 2d 1286 (1971)

*Hobson v. Hansen*, 265 F. Supp. 902 (Feb. 9, 1967) aff'd 269 F. Supp. 401 (June 19, 1967)

*Hudgens v. National Labor Relations Board*, 424 U.S. 507 (1976)

*Jackson v. Choate*, 404 F. 2d 910 (1968)

*James v. Valtierra*, 402 U.S. 137 (1971)

*Jefferson v. Hackney*, 406 U.S. 535 (1972)

*Kramer v. Union School District*, 395 U.S. 621 (1969)

*Maher v. Roe*, 432 U.S. 464 (1977)

McDonald v. Board of Election Commissioners of Chicago, 394 U.S. 802 (1969)

McInnis v. Shapiro, 293 F. Supp. 327 (1968) aff'd McInnis v. Oglive, 394 U.S. 322 (1969)

Miller v. Korns, 107 Ohio St. 287 (1923)

Milliken v. Bradley, 418 U.S. 717 (1974)

Oregon v. Mitchell, 400 U.S. 112 (1970)

Parker v. Mandel, 344 F. Supp. 1068 (D. Md. 1972)

Pierce v. Society of Sisters, 268 U.S. 510 (1925)

Plessy v. Ferguson, 163 U.S. 537 (1896)

Robinson v. Cahill, 62 N.J. 473 (1973)

Roe v. Wade, 410 U.S. 113 (1973)

Serrano v. Priest
5 Cal. 3d 584 (1971) (Serrano I)
18 Cal. 3d 728 (1976) (Serrano II)

Shapiro v. Thompson, 394 U.S. 618 (1969)

State ex rel. State v. Lewis, 98 Ohio St. 3d 1509 (2003)

Texas v. Mitchell, 400 U.S. 112 (1970)

United States v. Carolene Products, 304 U.S. 144 (1938)

United States v. Guest, 383 U.S. 745 (1966)

Van Dusartz v. Hatfield, 334 F. Supp. 870 (D. Minn. 1971)

*Note from the series editors: The following bibliographical essay contains the primary and secondary sources the author consulted for this volume. We have asked all authors in the series to omit formal citations in order to make our volumes more readable, inexpensive, and appealing for students and general readers. In adopting this format, Landmark Law Cases and American Society follows the precedent of a number of highly regarded and widely consulted series.*

Whenever possible, I made use of primary source material to research this book. I spent several days at the National Archives and Records Administration branch in Fort Worth, Texas, reading and copying the depositions, affidavits, trial records, and trial transcripts from the initial hearings before the three-judge district court. Of particular interest were files from district judge Adrian Spears, which contained not only relevant legal records but also letters, telephone messages, and newspaper clippings from the period surrounding the *Rodriguez* decision. Moving to the U.S. Supreme Court phase of the case, my account of the *Rodriguez* deliberations of the Court and the chambers of Justice Powell is based upon materials in the *San Antonio v. Rodriguez* case file at the Lewis F. Powell, Jr., Archives at Washington and Lee University School of Law in Lexington, Virginia. Documents from the Powell archives were supplemented by the William O. Douglas and Thurgood Marshall papers. I was able to review both collections at the Library of Congress Manuscript Division in Washington, D.C. As others who have written for this series have noted, much that goes on inside the walls of the Supreme Court building is shielded from the public. This is particularly true of conference discussions, where even the clerks are not present. Although I have tried my best to recreate the conversations that occurred, the accounts necessarily depend upon the accuracy of the notes taken by the actual participants.

As it turned out, information on the background of the case was perhaps even more difficult to come by than Supreme Court records. Fortunately, in March of 2004, I was able to meet with Demetrio Rodriguez at his home to discuss his recollections about the case. While in San Antonio, I also spoke over the phone with Manuel Garza, one of the students involved in the Edgewood High School walk-out I described in Chapter 2. Over the past few years, I have exchanged phone calls and many e-mail messages with Arthur Gochman, the lawyer who argued *Rodriguez* before the three-judge district court in Texas and the U.S. Supreme Court. Mark Yudof, who worked on the *Rodriguez* briefs with Gochman, allowed me to interview him over the phone in July of 2005. Among the most helpful newspaper accounts of the events surrounding both *Rodriguez* and *Serrano v. Priest* (1971) (the California school funding case that was decided during the same period), are Robert Reinhold, "John Serrano Jr., et al., and School Tax Equality," *New York Times,* January 10, 1972, p. 1-E, and William Geider, "Novel Theory of School Spending Cashiered by the Court," *Washington Post,* March 22, 1973, p. 16-A.

A transcript of the Supreme Court oral arguments in *Rodriguez* as well as copies of many of the briefs are available in Philip B. Kurland and Gerhard Casper, eds., *Landmark Briefs and Arguments of the Supreme Court of the United States: Constitutional Law,* vol. 76 (Arlington, VA: University Publications of America, 1975). The oral argument transcript does not indicate which justice asked a particular question. By combining the transcript with the audio recording of the oral argument, available online at the *Oyez Project* (www.oyez.org/oyez/frontpage), I was able to determine with some degree of certainty which justice was speaking at that point in the hearing.

As I prepared to write this book, I read many judicial biographies. Of particular importance to *Rodriguez* are John C. Jeffries, Jr., *Justice Lewis F. Powell, Jr.* (New York: Fordham University Press, 2001) and Carl T. Rowan, *Dream Makers, Dream Breakers: The World of Justice Thurgood Marshall* (New York: Welcome Rain, 2002). In addition to the justices, another important participant in *Rodriguez* was the late Charles Alan Wright, who represented the State of Texas before the Supreme Court. Roy M. Mersky has edited an excellent volume entitled *Charles Alan Wright: The Man and the Scholar* (Austin and Minneapolis: Jamail Legal Research Center and West Group, 2000).

Many articles and book chapters analyze the legal reasoning in *Rodriguez.* A sampling includes the following: David A. J. Richards, "Equal Opportunity and School Financing: Towards a Moral Theory of Constitutional Adjudication," *University of Chicago Law Review* 41 (1973): 32; Judith Areen and Leonard Ross, *The Rodriguez Case: Judicial Oversight of School Finance in the* Supreme Court Review, *1973* (Chicago: University of Chicago Press, 1974), p. 33; John E. Coons, "Introduction: 'Fiscal Neutrality' after *Rodriguez,*" *Law and Contemporary Problems* 38 (Winter-Spring 1974): 299; J. Harvie Wilkinson, III, "The Three Faces of Constitutional Equality," *Virginia Law Review* 61 (1975): 945; Cass R. Sunstein, *The Partial Constitution* (Boston: Harvard University Press, 1993); Erwin Chemerinsky, "Lost Opportunity: The Burger Court and the Failure to Achieve Equal Educational Opportunity," *Mercer Law Review* 45 (1997): 999; and Edward B. Foley, "*Rodriguez* Revisited: Constitutional Theory and School Finance," *Georgia Law Review* 32 (1998): 475. As mentioned in the preface, Peter Irons also dedicates two chapters to *Rodriguez* in *The Courage of their Convictions* (New York: The Free Press, 1988).

The Montesquieu quotes in Chapter 1 are from *The Spirit of the Laws,* David Wallace Carrithers, ed. (Berkeley: University of California Press, 1977). For a general background on public education in the United States, see H. G. Good,

*A History of American Education*, New York: Macmillan, 1956), R.F. Butts, *Public Education in the United States: From Revolution to Reform* (New York: Holt, Rinehart, and Winston, 1978), and E. I. F. Williams, *Horace Mann: Educational Statesman* (New York: Macmillan, 1937). More specific information about the history of segregated education in the District of Columbia is provided by Constance McLaughlin Green in *Washington: Village and Capital, 1800–1878* (Princeton, NJ: Princeton University Press, 1962). For an introduction to the development of the school funding system in Texas, the description at the beginning of Justice Powell's majority opinion in *Rodriguez* is well supplemented by Mark G. Yudof and Daniel C. Morgan, "*Rodriguez v. San Antonio Independent School District:* Gathering the Ayes of Texas — The Politics of School Finance Reform," *Law and Contemporary Problems* 38 (Winter-Spring 1974). Those with an interest in Mexican American education and politics should see Guadalupe San Miguel, Jr., *Let All of Them Take Heed: Mexican Americans and the Campaign for Educational Equality in Texas, 1910–1981* (Austin: University of Texas Press, 1987), and, of course, Carey McWilliams's classic *North from Mexico* (Westport, CT: Greenwood, 1990). I also used information from the Web site of the Mexican American Legal Defense and Educational Fund (www.maldef.org/about/founding.htm), the American GI Forum (www.agif.us/aboutus.htm), and the League of United Latin American Citizens (www.lulac.org/about/history.html).

As explained throughout the book, *Rodriguez* was significant not only because of its impact on school funding law, but also because of its influence on equal protection jurisprudence. Walter F. Murphy, James E. Fleming, Sotirious A. Barber, and Stephen Macedo offer an overview of the issues surrounding interpretation of the Equal Protection Clause in *American Constitutional Interpretation*, 3rd ed. (New York: Foundation Press 2003), especially in Chapters 14 and 15. My discussion of the *Carolene Products* case was guided by Louis Luskey, "The *Carolene Products* Footnote" in *The Encyclopedia of the American Constitution* (New York: The Free Press, 1981). Interestingly enough, I discovered a copy of this article in one of Justice Powell's office files.

No one can intelligently discuss the legal decisions involving the financing of public education without relying on the works of John E. Coons, William H. Clune III, and Stephen D. Sugarman. Their seminal work is *Private Wealth and Public Education* (Cambridge, MA: Belknap Press of Harvard University, 1970). George Clowes did an interview with Coons that I found very helpful in the February 1, 2001 issue of *School Reform News*, available at http://heartland.org/Article.cfm?artId=10213. For more contemporary studies of school funding with an emphasis on the role of state courts, the reader should consult Stephen Macedo, "School Reform and Equal Opportunity in America's Geography of Inequality," *Perspectives on Politics* 1, no. 4 (December 2003): 743; Douglas S. Reed, *On Equal Terms: Constitutional Politics of Educational Opportunity* (Princeton, NJ: Princeton University Press, 2001); and Abigail Thernstrom and Stephen Thernstrom, *No Excuses: Closing the Racial Gap in Learning* (New York: Simon and Schuster, 2003).

Gerald Gunther's article, referred to in Chapter 3 and discussed in Chapter 8, is "In Search of Evolving Doctrine on a Changing Court: A Model for a Newer Equal Protection," *Harvard Law Review* 86, no. 1 (November 1972): 1. The *Yale Law Journal* article on school funding published shortly before oral arguments in Rodriguez and discussed during those arguments as well as in the majority and dissenting opinions is "A Statistical Analysis of the School Finance Decisions: On Winning Battles and Losing Wars," *Yale Law Journal* 81 (July 1972): 1303. William Brennan's article on judicial federalism, mentioned at the beginning of Chapter 10, is "State Constitutions and the Protection of Individual Rights," *Harvard Law Review* 90: 489.

Two of the best sources for basic information about the law and the Supreme Court are Walter F. Murphy, C. Herman Pritchett, and Lee Epstein, *Courts, Judges, and Politics: An Introduction to the Judicial Process*, 5th ed. (New York: McGraw Hill, 2002), and David M. O'Brien, *Storm Center: The Supreme Court and American Politics*, 7th ed. (New York: Norton, 2005). Other books in the "Landmark Cases" series, especially Robert J. Controll, Raymond T. Diamond, and Leland Ware, Brown v. Board of Education (Lawrence: University Press of Kansas, 2003) and Howard Ball, *The* Bakke *Case: Race, Education, and Affirmative Action* (Lawrence: University Press of Kansas, 2000), provide excellent context for understanding *Rodriguez*.

Finally, one of the most confusing legal elements in *Rodriguez* concerns the complex rules (which have since changed) governing when a three-judge district court may be convened. The preeminent authority on this and other jurisdictional issues is Charles Alan Wright, *Law of the Federal Courts*, 4th ed. (St. Paul, MN: West, 1983).